Cultural Change

JEWISH, CHRISTIAN, AND ISLAMIC

COINS OF THE HOLY LAND

This is book number __79__ of

the first 250 copies of the first printing.

11/9/11

To Frederic
   with appreciation
   + best wishes —

Cultural Change

Jewish, Christian, and Islamic Coins of the Holy Land

Featuring coins from the Abraham D. & Marian Scheuer Sofaer Collection

David Hendin

AMERICAN NUMISMATIC SOCIETY
75 VARICK STREET, FLOOR 11
NEW YORK, NY 10013

ISBN-10: 0-89722-319-5
ISBN-13: 978-0-89722-319-5

1 2 3 4 5 6 7 8 9 0

Printed in Mexico

TABLE OF CONTENTS

INTRODUCTION & ACKNOWLEDGEMENTS

This book has been created to accompany the exhibit *CULTURAL CHANGE: Coins of the Holy Land*, created by the American Numismatic Society (ANS) and first shown at the Museum of the Federal Reserve Bank of New York from May 2011 to February 2012. The exhibit has been created around the collection of Abraham D. Sofaer, who, with his wife Marion, has donated many of the coins to the ANS and the Israel Museum. The remainder of the collection is on long-term loan to the ANS at this time. The Foreword, followed by a brief section on the Sofaer Collection will explain much more about my long-time friendship with him and the principles by which he created his collection.

I have organized the book so it serves as an independent introduction to the topic of Jewish, Christian, and Islamic coins of the Holy Land, which for our purpose includes the lands of ancient Judaea, Samaria, the Galilee, Trans-Jordan, and some nearby lands. I have chronologically discussed the coins of the Jews, coins used by Jesus during his life, the rise of Christianity as a state-sponsored religion in Rome, Islamic coins minted in the area, and coins of Crusader Jerusalem.

Jerusalem is one of the most storied cities of all time and a great deal of its history is connected to these coinages. In turn, the coins portray Jerusalem in different ways, and a section of this book describes and illustrates how the city was named and depicted on coins from its earliest numismatic issues through the Crusades.

Roman provincial coins struck at the cities of the ancient Holy Land reflect the culture of each city and their various religious, historic, and geographic influences, and also serve as circulating "advertisements" for the features of each city. These topics are illustrated and discussed in the section on the gods, goddesses, and monuments that are displayed on these coins.

This volume is not intended to be a comprehensive on the subjects of Judaean and Biblical coins, which would require far more space. But it is an introduction to these fascinating topics and toward that end I have also provided a brief synopsis of the field of Biblical/Judaean coins, family trees of the Maccabees and Herodians, and, perhaps most importantly, a list of some of the books I recommend for those who may be interested in further pursuing one or more of these topics.

Neither the exhibit nor the book would have been possible without help from many exceptional people.

ANS executive director Ute Wartenberg Kagan and ANS deputy

director Andy Meadows are both former curators of Greek coins at the British Museum, and their assistance was invaluable.

Andy nurtured the project, edited the book, and finalized the publishing process. Ute discovered among the ANS treasures a wonderful book from the mid-1800s filled with images of the Holy Land taken by photographer Felix Bonfils, some of which are shown here.

ANS museum administrator Joanne Isaac has assisted in every step of the process, from editing to designing graphics, not to mention almost any other chore that needed to be done.

The Sofaer collection at the American Numismatic Society contains thousands of coins. Locating them and removing them properly would have been an impossible task without ANS collections manager Elena Stolyarik. Not only does she know the locations of most of the more than 800,000 coins and related objects in ANS collections, but she patiently explained the procedures for removing coins for exhibit and recording what they are and where they have been taken.

Other ANS colleagues, including Michael Bates, Robert Hoge, Rick Witschonke, Sylvia Karges, Julian Biber, and Anouska Hamlin, double checked material, helped with inventory, record keeping and various jobs too numerous to be listed here. ANS photographer Alan Roche created superb images of each of the coins and objects we selected for the exhibit and this catalog. Special graphics on pages 89, 115, 116 were created with the assistance of J.P. Fontanille; Shayna Blumenthal designed the covers and interiors.

We were not at all worried about the security at New York Federal Reserve Bank, since in addition to the ANS permanent exhibit and the *CULTURAL CHANGE* exhibit, they protect the largest single stash of gold in the entire world—more than Ft. Knox! Our host at "The Fed" was Official Curator of the New York Federal Reserve Bank Rosemary Lazenby and her fabulous staff, who greeted us each day and took care of all of the questions and needs particular to this installation.

We also thank Michal Dayagi-Mendels and Haim Gitler of The Israel Museum, Jerusalem, who have kindly allowed the ANS to temporarily retain some of the coins donated to their museum by Abraham and Marion Sofaer, in order to include them in this exhibit.

I couldn't complete a project without offering sincere thanks to my wife Jeannie, my children Sarah and Robert Cohen, Ben and Chrissy Hendin, and Alexander Hendin, and my grandsons Max and Charlie Cohen. They are alway good humored and supportive when a supposedly retired husband, father, and grandfather is off curating, excavating, researching, or writing just *one more* project.

FOREWORD

When I first met Abraham Sofaer around 1981, I had no idea how long our friendship would last, or how interesting it would become. We first met one day in around 1981, when I was visiting the Jewish Museum in New York, and chairman of the Museum Richard J. Scheuer, also Sofaer's father-in-law, walked by. Scheuer spotted me, called me over, and introduced me to Abe. Sofaer had expressed an interest in ancient Jewish coins, and Scheuer wanted us to know each other because of that common interest.

At the time, I was chairman the Jewish Museum's numismatic committee and I was working with the late Ya'akov Meshorer in creating an exhibit of ancient biblical coins called *Coins Reveal*.

I had no idea that Sofaer would spend more than 30 years building one of the best private collections of coins of the ancient Holy Land ever assembled. He and his wife Marion last year donated to the ANS his remarkable collection of coins of Samaria (more than 260 coins), the Jewish War (55 coins), and the Bar Kokhba Revolt (171 coins). The Sofaers also donated part of the collection to the Israel Museum and plan to donate more to these two institutions in the future.

Sofaer and I have remained friends since we first met, and it was with great pleasure that I recently found myself as curator of the exhibit upon which this catalog is based.

With seven large cabinets containing more than 300 coins and related objects, it is possibly the largest exhibit of ancient coins from the Holy Land that has ever been launched outside of Israel. By comparison the current elegant coin room at the Israel Museum displays 54 coins and the Jewish Museum's *Coins Reveal* exhibit in 1983 contained around 200 coins, but only half of them were ancient. More important than size, however, is that the focus of this exhibit, like Sofaer's stellar collection, reflects a cultural dimension of the Holy Land.

Sofaer's passion for these coins stems from his interest in the Holy Land, both ancient and modern. In the introduction to the book cataloging his collection, soon to be published by the ANS, Sofaer mentions some of his high-level involvement, as well as a political comment: "I was privileged as the U.S. State Department Legal Adviser to have served as principal negotiator of the agreement between Egypt and Israel that settled their boundary at Taba. Peace agreements must be achieved between Israel and all of its neighboring people."

Sofaer collected on a personal level, becoming close friends with key numismatists in Israel such as Ya'akov Meshorer, principal author of the corpus of Sofaer's collection, and Shraga Qedar, co-author with Meshorer of two volumes on Samarian coinage. The donations of Sofaer's collections to both the ANS and the Israel Museum were made in Meshorer's memory. Meshorer, who died in 2004, was recipient of the ANS Huntington Medal in 2001. In addition to academics and curators, Sofaer befriended many of Israel's licensed coin dealers, as well as many collectors. In his introduction to the book of his collection, Sofaer talks about some of these colorful individuals such as Meir Rosenberger, "a tailor who, with very little money, painstakingly put together a huge collection of city coins, which he published in four volumes. He was an avid and knowledgeable collector, and a gentle and intelligent man, whom everyone liked and admired."

Fig. i. Abu-Salah Club button c. 1980. David Hendin collection.

Sofaer also recalls a favorite dealer, George Momjian, who had a shop near the Muristan in Jerusalem's Old City for decades. "No one took the rituals of civility more seriously than this Armenian gentleman. Anyone who lacked the patience and good taste to appreciate Momjian's company might never see any of his coins, and certainly not his best. I spent hours with him, playing backgammon, drinking coffee, and eating meals delivered from a local restaurant. During these visits, he would suddenly get up and rummage through drawers and packages to find some interesting coins to show me. Unlike other dealers, Momjian never charged inflated prices, and virtually never reduced them. One bargained with him during the verbal sparring that preceded any offer to buy or sell, by making comments aimed at pushing up or down the item's value." Sofaer the professional State Department negotiator further observes that "This is a subtle form of negotiation, in which the most knowledgeable do best, which gave Momjian the advantage. His first son was named Salah, so, as is customary in the Middle East, he was called Abu Salah (*Father of Salah*). An inner circle of aficionados formed what we called the Abu Salah Club. Someone made up buttons, which we continued to wear when we got together, even long after he died and the shop was sold."

Sofaer's concludes: "While I started out primarily interested in Jewish coins, I soon realized that the Holy Land presented an opportunity to collect coins minted in a single small area, by no fewer than ten civilizations: Persians; Greeks; Hebrews; Samarians; Nabataeans; Romans; Byzantines; Arabs; Crusaders, and Israelis. Vast differences exist, moreover, even among the Jewish coins minted in the area; some are very Hebrew, with no images of people or gods, while others bear the portraits of emperors and pagan gods. The coins minted in the area reflect the long history of Jews in the Holy land, but also the long, multi-cultural, historical parade of other peoples. The Holy Land is important to many peoples, in addition to the Jews; and every effort by one cultural group to dominate the area to the exclusion of others eventually failed. A stable future for the Holy Land requires a commitment by all groups in the area to maintaining multi-cultural and tolerant regimes."

Fig. ii. Abu-Salah Club meeting at the Hendin home c. 1980, back row from l. William Stern, Leo Mildenberg, Herb Kreindler, Ya'akov Meshorer; front row from l. Abraham Sofaer, David Hendin, Robert Schonwalter. Photograph by Don Simon.

The Sofaer Collection

Most of the coins in this book and the exhibit upon which it is based belong to the Sofaer Collection of coins of the Holy Land at the American Numismatic Society, New York, and The Israel Museum.

Abraham D. Sofaer has been a collector of Holy Land coins for more than thirty years. He and his wife Marian Scheuer Sofaer recently decided to donate the collection to these two institutions. Abe Sofaer is a former Federal District Judge of the Southern District of New York. He was Legal Adviser to the U.S. State Department under Secretaries of State George P. Shultz and James A. Baker, III. He is currently the George P. Shultz Senior Fellow at the Hoover Institution, Stanford University.

In assembling this collection, Sofaer sought a multi-cultural selection that includes the ancient Jewish coins, Christian coins of the Byzantine and Crusader Periods, and Islamic coins minted in the area. The collection ranges from the fifth century BCE to the thirteenth century CE and includes some of the greatest rarities of the series.

Reflecting on his collection, Sofaer notes that "These coins represent a geographic area that is unique in the totality of its cultural and ideological variety and significance. The Holy Land has been fought over by various empires for some 3,000 years. The Holy Land has almost always been a province of one of the area's major empires, since about the sixth century BCE, when coins were first minted there, until the State of Israel was declared. But it has been a province rich in human drama, social and political upheaval, cultural and religious diversity, commerce, and creativity. Consequently, while lacking the military, political, artistic, and economic dominance of the empires which controlled it, Holy Land numismatics is intellectually and artistically rewarding."

The Ancient Shekel

Shekel is one of the oldest known names for a unit of precious weight or currency. The first recorded use of the word was in Akkadian, around 2150 BCE, when it was called a *siqlu*. The shekel (also transliterated as sheqel) was mentioned in the Code of Hammurabi in 1700 BCE.

Many civilizations and geographic areas of the ancient Near East used the shekel as their principal currency unit, although each region's shekel was based upon a slightly different weight standard. The first documented biblical real estate transaction occurred when Abraham bought the Cave of Machpelah in Hebron, to use as a family burial site, from Ephron the Hittite. This took place before coins were invented, and the shekel referred to was a unit of weight.

> And Abraham weighed to Ephron … four hundred shekels
> of silver current money with the merchant – GENESIS 23:16.

Shekels and half-shekels of the Phoenician city of Tyre were prominently used in the ancient Holy Land. They were minted between 126 BCE and about 66 CE, and were the only coins accepted in payment for the annual half-shekel tax due from each Jewish man at the Jerusalem Temple. During the Jewish War against Rome, from 66 to 70 CE, purely Jewish shekels were minted in Jerusalem until the Temple was destroyed. The shekel has become the most storied denomination of money in history. Today, the word shekel commonly refers to money or cash. The monetary system of the state of Israel is also based on the shekel.

The word shekel only begins to describe the fascination of the ancient coins of Biblical times. The coins in this exhibit have been preserved by the parched climate of the Holy Land for some 2,000 years and then brought to light and given new life, not as "coin of the realm," but as a key to the mind. The doors this key can open are limited only by imagination.

Before Coins Were Invented

Coins as we know them were invented in Western Asia Minor between 650 and 600 BCE. The first method of exchange was barter, frequently using livestock as a principal currency. Later, metals became the standard currency, and gold, silver, and bronze were most commonly used.

Small silver ingots hacked from larger cast chunks have been documented in the ancient Holy Land as early as the Middle Bronze Age (2200 – 1550 BCE). Use of these small silver ingots, often including bits of silver jewelry and chopped pieces of foreign silver coins, became a unified form of payment during the Iron Age (1000 – 586 BCE) in the Holy Land. During this pre-coinage period, some of the cut pieces may have already adhered to standard weights.

The Hebrew word for money in the Bible is *kesef*, which means silver, referring to these small ingots. Throughout the ancient Near East it was common to weigh these on balance scales against stones of known weight. For hundreds of years, cut coins and bits of silver were weighed alongside coins as a method of payment. Eventually people developed more confidence in stamped (struck) coins and this tradition disappeared.

And Abraham weighed to Ephron the silver – GENESIS 23:16.

1   2

1. Judean stone *Netzef* weight, about 9.4 grams, 8th – 6th centuries BCE.

    Courtesy private collection.

2. Silver cut ingot, c. 6th century BCE.
    ANS Collection: ANS 2005.12.17.

3. Balance scale similar to scales used in the biblical period,
    3rd century BCE – 1st century CE.
    Courtesy private collection.

Fig. 1.   Using a balance scale with bull-shaped weights and round ingots;
from a tomb in Thebes, Egypt, c. 1400 BCE. After the original.

JEWISH HISTORY ON COINS

The coins struck in the ancient Holy Land between the fourth century BCE and the second century CE provide a primary source of information about the history, heritage, and emerging culture of the Judeo-Christian tradition. Coins witnessed the return of Jews from the Babylonian captivity, the wars of the Maccabees with the kings of Seleucid Syria, the building and destruction of the Second Temple in Jerusalem, the birth and ascent of Christianity, and the creation of Rabbinic Judaism.

Gold Coin of the Bible

When mentioned in the Old Testament, the shekel is a weight, not a coin. But the daric, mentioned in Chronicles I (29:7), Ezra (2:69, 8:27) and Nehemiah (7:70–72) was a circulating coin through the fifth and fourth centuries BCE in the western Persian Empire.

> I will give all Judah into the hand of the king of Babylon,
> and he shall carry them captive to Babylon – JEREMIAH 20: 4.

It would thus seem likely that many darics were carried back to the ancient Holy Land by the returning Jews, who must have used them. However, until today only one daric and two gold double darics have been found in controlled archaeological excavations in Judaea, Philistia, Samaria, and the Galilee.

> They gave after their ability into the treasury of the work threescore and one thousand darics of gold, and five thousand pounds of silver, and one hundred priests' tunics – EZRA 2:69.

4
2:1

4. Persia, Achaemenid Empire gold daric, time of Darius I to Xerxes II, 485 – 420 BCE.

    Obverse: Persian king or hero kneeling to right, holding spear and bow, quiver over shoulder.

    Reverse: Incuse punch.

    ANS Collection: 1944.100.73489.

Coins of Samaria (Shomron), late 4ᵗʰ century BCE

The history of coins of Samaria (*Shomron* in Hebrew and Aramaic) and Judah (*Yehud*), to the south, began at the end of the Persian Period. Samarian coins were minted between around 375 – 333 BCE. Aside from the coins, several references in the biblical books of Ezra, Nehemiah, and Chronicles, and a few manuscripts, history knows little of these years. It is generally believed that at around 400 BCE the Samaritans were still considered Jewish.

The final separation between the Samaritans and the Jews probably evolved in the years before Alexander the Great conquered the area (around 332 BCE). According to the Roman historian Josephus, it was Manasseh, a member of the high priest's family in Jerusalem, who left for Samaria, married Nikaso the daughter of Sanballat, the governor of Samaria, and became the high priest of the newly built Samaritan Temple on Mt. Gerizim.

Samaria issued silver coins to maintain parallel prestige with cities in Judah, Phoenicia, and Philistia. The small silver coins filled needs for small payments in religious, military, and commercial transactions.

> He bought the hill of Samaria of Shemer for two talents of silver; and he built on the hill and called the name of the city which he built, after the name of Shemer, the owner of the hill, Samaria — I KINGS 16: 24.

5
2:1

6

5. Samarian silver ma'ah-obol, 375 – 333 BCE, 0.72 g.

    Obverse: וש (s[mry]n—Shomron) in l. field; Persian king sitting on throne r., wearing jagged crown and long folded garment, holding knotted scepter in l. hand and smelling flower held in his r.

    Reverse: זמ (mz—Mazdai) in l. field; crowned, bearded and four-winged deity with bird's tail, r., holding flower in r. hand and uncertain object in l.

    The name Mazdai probably refers to Mazaeus (died 328 BCE), a Persian nobleman and governor of Babylon, the last governor of Cilicia.
    ANS Collection: 2010.77.41. Gift of Abraham and Marion Sofaer.

6. Samarian silver quarter-shekel, 375 – 333 BCE, 4.08 g.

    Obverse: ד (ד, d) above horse walking l., all in a dotted square border.

    Reverse: ד (ד, d) above winged sphinx with head of Persian king l., all in dotted square border.

    The letter D could abbreviate the name Delayah, used in the Bible in the time frame of the sixth to fifth centuries BCE. It is also the name of one of the sons of Sanballat, governor of Samaria, mentioned in letters from Elephantine in Egypt. He may have succeeded his father as governor early in the fourth century BCE. Meaning of the name is "healed by the Lord" as used in Psalms 30:2.
    ANS Collection: 2010.77.11. Gift of Abraham and Marion Sofaer.

7
2:1

7. Samarian silver quarter-shekel, 375 – 333 BCE, 3.58 g.

    Obverse: Two confronted heads, the l. one bearded and male, the r. one female; the female wearing a pearled diadem and a necklace, the male wearing a necklace; border of dots.

    Reverse: Male bearded head r., wearing headgear shaped like a lion's protome and a necklace; in l. field ש (ש, S).

    The letter S may abbreviate Shomron, although both sides of this coin resemble Philistian issues rather than Samarian ones.
    ANS Collection: 2010.77.258. Gift of Abraham and Marion Sofaer.

Coins of Judah (Yehud)

Yehud was the Persian name of the province of Judah. Many Jewish people returned to Judah after the Babylonian exile. They rebuilt its capital, Jerusalem, and the Temple. We read about this episode of history in the books of Ezra and Nehemiah. Not all of the Jews had been taken to Babylon. Those who remained behind retained Hebrew as their language, but the Jews who returned from Babylon began speaking Aramaic, which soon became the dominant language, not only in Judah, but throughout most of the ancient Levant.

Hebrew continued to be used mainly on the coins of Yehud, and on some official seals and documents. This was a graphic exhibition of nationalistic pride and religious tradition. The earliest Yehud coins were struck under the Persian authorities, while the latest ones were struck under the rule of the Ptolemaic Kings of Egypt.

The coins of Yehud were minted from around 400 to 260 BCE The earliest denomination of the Yehud coins is thought to be the gerah, or 1/20 of a shekel, which is mentioned in the Bible (Exodus 30: 13).

8
2:1

9
2:1

8. Yehud silver gerah, before 333 BCE, 0.50 g.
    Obverse: Helmeted head of Athena r., decorated with olive wreath.
    Reverse: יהד (*yhd*) to r. of owl standing to r., head facing, small lily above l.
    Courtesy The Abraham D. Sofaer Collection on loan at the ANS.

9. Yehud silver half-gerah, before 333 BCE, 0.31 g.
    Obverse: Lily.
    Reverse: יהד (*yhd*) above r. wing of falcon with wings spread, head r.
    Courtesy The Abraham D. Sofaer Collection on loan at the ANS.

10
2:1

11
2:1

10. Yehud silver half-gerah, before 333 BCE, 0.27 g.
    Obverse: Head of Persian king wearing jagged crown facing r.
    Reverse: ו‎ﬤ‎ﬡ (‏יהד‎, *yhd*) to r. of falcon, wings spread, head r.
    Courtesy The Abraham D. Sofaer Collection on loan at the ANS.

11. Yehud half ma'ah-obol, before 333 BCE, 0.32 g.
    Obverse: Facing head in a circle of connected dots.
    Reverse: ﬡﬨ‎ו‎ﬡ (‏הפחה‎, *hapecha—the governor*) to l., ﬨ‎ﬡﬤ‎ﬨﬡﬨ‎
    (‏יחזקי ה‎, *yhzqyh—Hezekiah*) to r. of owl standing r., head facing,
    the feathers of the head form a beaded circle.
    Courtesy The Abraham D. Sofaer Collection on loan at the ANS.

12
2:1

13
2:1

12. Yehud silver hemidrachm (?), 285 – 274 BCE, 1.58 g.
    Obverse: Diademed head of Ptolemy I r.
    Reverse: ﬡﬠﬤﬡﬨ (‏יהדה‎, *yhdh*) to l. of eagle, wings spread, half
    turned l. and standing upon thunderbolt.
    Courtesy The Abraham D. Sofaer Collection on loan at the ANS.

13. Yehud silver quarter- ma'ah-obol, 285 – 274 BCE, 0.18 g.
    Obverse: Diademed head of Ptolemy I r.
    Reverse: ﬡﬠﬤﬡﬨ (‏יהדה‎, *yhdh*) to l. of eagle, wings spread, half
    turned l. and standing upon thunderbolt.
    Courtesy The Abraham D. Sofaer Collection on loan at the ANS.
    Both of the above coins are copied from larger silver coins of Ptolemy
        struck in Egypt.

Seleucid Coin of Antiochus IV (175 to 164 BCE)

The ancient Holy Land was fought over by the Seleucid Kings of Syria and the Ptolemaic Kings of Egypt, and changed hands many times. By 198 BCE, when Antiochus III defeated the boy-king Ptolemy V, the Jews had become fed up with the rule of the Ptolemies. They welcomed Antiochus III to Jerusalem and he rewarded them by rescinding taxes, making contributions to the Temple, and rebuilding portions of the city.

Thus it was a dramatic turn of events when Antiochus III's son, Antiochus IV (175 – 164 BCE) forced Greek culture and religion upon the Jews and caused a major turning point in Jewish history. On his coins, Antiochus IV proclaimed himself "God Made Manifest" but he was mocked by some as "Antiochus the Mad." He prohibited worship of the Jewish God, burned the Torah, and defiled the Temple by sacrificing a sow on the holy altar. The Jewish people initiated the holiday of Chanukah when the Maccabees defeated Antiochus IV in 166 BCE and the Jerusalem Temple was re-purified. Chanukah is still celebrated by Jews worldwide each year more than 2,000 years later.

14

14. Antiochus IV (175 – 164 BCE) silver tetradrachm, struck at Akko-Ptolemais.
    Obverse: Diademed head of Antiochus IV r., fillet border, ⚕ monogram behind head.
    Reverse: ΒΑΣΙΛΕΩΣ ΑΝΤΙΟΧΟΥ ΘΕΟΥ ΕΠΙΦΑΝΟΥΣ ΝΙΚΗΦΟΡΟΥ *(of King Antiochus, god made manifest, bringer of victory)*; Zeus seated l. on throne, holds Nike and scepter, palm branch to far left, various control marks in exergue or on left.
    Courtesy The Abraham D. Sofaer Collection on loan at the ANS.

Graven Images on Coins

In contrast to the coins of the Greeks and Romans, which commonly use the portraits of rulers and other graven images of creatures or gods, most of the coins struck under Jewish rulers in ancient times follow the biblical code prohibiting graven images as stated in Exodus 20:4:

> Thou shalt not make unto thee a graven image, nor any manner of likeness, of anything that is in heaven above, or that is in the earth beneath, or that is in the water under the earth.

Thus Jewish rulers of the Maccabean and Herodian Dynasties in Judaea issued coins that served their nation's economy, but also made bold statements regarding their sovereignty while maintaining the understanding of this Jewish religious law at the time. The first coins struck by the Maccabean rulers beginning around 130 BCE carried a paleo-Hebrew inscription with the name of the ruler within a laurel wreath. The wreath was associated with leadership and royalty in the Hellenistic and Roman worlds. The Maccabees, followed by Herod I, also adopted the cornucopia to signify the abundance of the land; the pomegranate, a symbol of fertility; and the lily, a symbol of their capital, Jerusalem. The anchor, galley, and other symbols were soon added.

The first graven image to appear on a coin struck by a Jewish king was the eagle on a coin of Herod I (40 – 4 BCE). His son Herod Philip (4 BCE – 34 CE), who did not rule in territories with a large Jewish population, was the first Jewish king to have his own portrait appear on his coins. Jewish coinage during the revolts against Rome resumed using religious symbols and avoided graven images.

Most Islamic coins minted in the Holy Land also avoided using graven images when they were minted beginning in the seventh century CE and they used only holy inscriptions and few images of any kind.

COINS OF THE MACCABEES

15

16

15. John Hyrcanus I (135 – 104 BCE) bronze prutah with the name of Antiochus VII, struck 131/130 BCE, struck in Jerusalem.
Obverse: Lily.
Reverse: ΒΑΣΙΛΕΩΣ ΑΝΤΙΟΧΟΥ ΕΥΕΡΓΕΤΟΥ (*of King Antiochus, benefactor*); inverted anchor, below anchor ΒΠΡ (SE 182 = 131/130 BCE).

The first Maccabean coin was struck with the approval and name of Antiochus VII, who had granted the Jews privileges, including the right to coin money with their own stamp, to maintain their friendship. This coin may have been among the first struck under the Maccabean mint in Jerusalem
Courtesy The Abraham D. Sofaer Collection on loan at the ANS.

16. John Hyrcanus I bronze prutah.
Obverse: "A" above paleo-Hebrew within wreath
(יהוחנן הכהן הגדל וחבר היהודים, *Yehohanan the High Priest and the Council of the Jews*).
Reverse: Double cornucopia adorned with ribbons, pomegranate between horns.
Courtesy The Abraham D. Sofaer Collection on loan at the ANS.

17

18

17. Alexander Jannaeus (104 – 76 BCE) bronze prutah.
Obverse: Lily flanked by paleo-Hebrew border of dots (המלך יהונתן, *Yehonatan the King*).
Reverse: ΒΑΣΙΛΕΩΣ ΑΛΕΞΑΝΔΡΟΥ (*of King Alexander*); inverted anchor within circle.
Courtesy The Abraham D. Sofaer Collection on loan at the ANS.

18. Alexander Jannaeus bronze prutah.
   Obverse: Paleo-Hebrew between the rays of star with eight rays within diadem (יהונתן המלך, *Yehonatan the King*).
   Reverse: ΒΑΣΙΛΕΩΣ ΑΛΕΞΑΝΔΡΟΥ *(of King Alexander)* around inverted anchor.
   Courtesy The Abraham D. Sofaer Collection on loan at the ANS.

19   20

19. Mattathias Antigonus (40 – 37 BCE) bronze 8 prutot.
   Obverse: Paleo-Hebrew; (מתתיה כהן הגדל חבר יד , *Mattatayah the High Priest and Council of the Jews*), around and between double cornucopia, some specimens have the letters נא, apparently retrograde for An[tigonus].
   Reverse: ΒΑCΙΛΕΩC ΑΝΤΙΓΟΝΟΥ *(of King Antigonus)* around ivy wreath tied with ribbons.
   Courtesy The Abraham D. Sofaer Collection on loan at the ANS.

20. Mattathias Antigonus bronze prutah.
   Obverse: Traces of paleo-Hebrew around showbread table (מתתיה כהן הגדל, *Mattatayah the High Priest*).
   Reverse: ΒΑΣΙΛΕΩΣ ΑΝΤΙΓΟΝΟΥ; seven-branched menorah.
   This small bronze prutah was struck under the last king and high priest of the Maccabean dynasty which governed ancient Israel from 152 to 37 BCE .Antigonus, backed by the Parthians, was locked in a battle with Herod I. Herod had been proclaimed King of the Jews by Rome in 40 BCE. That was also the first year of the rule of Antigonus, thus, Herod had been made king of a territory that already had a king. So, Herod and Antigonus went to war.
   Courtesy The Abraham D. Sofaer Collection on loan at the ANS.

Antigonus must have known that he was violating Jewish law against duplicating images of religious objects from the Jerusalem Temple when he ordered his mint to copy the menorah image onto this coin. It was an obvious propaganda tool and was certainly designed to rally the Jewish people to fight more vigorously to protect the sanctity of the

Temple and its high priest. The followers of the Maccabees considered it a sacrilege for Herod, an Idumaean (Edomite) Jew who was not from a priestly family, to become their ruler. Herod, however, claimed victory in 37 BCE.

The menorah coins of Mattathias Antigonus are among the most sought-after coins of the ancient Holy Land. Fewer than 30 examples are known to exist, and this is one of the best preserved.

The seven-branched menorah was central in the Jewish faith from the earliest times, and is described in the Old Testament:

> And you must make a lampstand of pure gold.... And you
> must make seven lamps for it; and the lamps must be lit up...
> – EXODUS 25: 31-40.

The Jewish priests (Kohens) in the Jerusalem Temple lit the golden menorah each evening, and cleaned it each morning, replacing the wicks and pouring fresh olive oil into its cups.

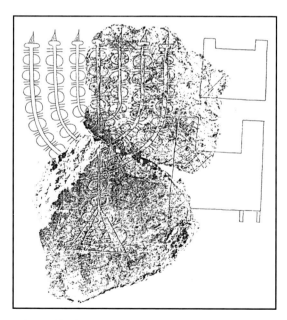

Fig. 2.   Menorah Graffiti (c. 30 BCE or earlier) were found scratched in the plaster wall of a first-century building in archaeological excavations of the Old City of Jerusalem. To the right of the menorah are two other objects. Image courtesy Dan Barag.

Antigonus' depiction of the menorah outside of the Jerusalem Temple was a violation of Jewish law. The Babylonian Talmud forbade making "a candelabrum after the design of the candelabrum [of the Temple]." Because of this prohibition, there are few images of the menorah known to have been made while the Second Temple stood; it was destroyed by the Romans in 70 CE.

This drawing of a menorah (Fig. 2) is one of very a few examples of the menorah produced in Jewish art while the Jerusalem Temple was still standing.

During this period the menorah was not intended as a symbol of Judaism itself, but a symbol of the Jerusalem Temple. After the Temple was destroyed in 70 CE, the menorah became a symbol of messianic hopes for rebuilding it, and was later adopted widely as a symbol of the Jewish faith.

Fig. 3.   Detail of the Arch of Titus, Rome, completed in 82 CE by Domitian after the death of his brother Titus. Photograph: David Hendin.

After the Roman troops under Titus destroyed the Jewish Temple, Jewish slaves and loot from Jerusalem were taken to Rome. The Temple's golden seven-branched menorah is featured among the captured artifacts shown in a bas-relief on the Arch of Titus, commemorating the Emperor's triumphal parade in Rome following the destruction of Jerusalem in 70 CE.

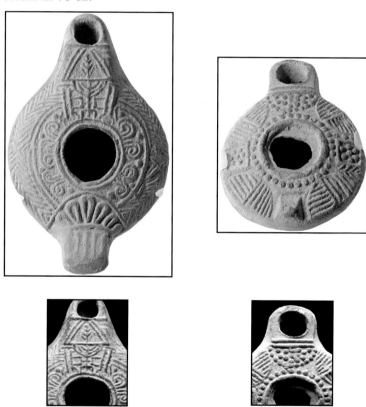

Fig. 4-5. Terra cotta oil lamps featuring the menorah, circa 3rd – 4th centuries CE found in Israel. Courtesy private collection.

Oil lamps that burned olive oil using braided wicks were sometimes decorated with the menorah as were other objects including, glass vessels, seals, and amulets as well as synagogue lintels, mosaics, and chancel screens. The menorah was also incised on sarcophagi and was painted, carved, and drawn on tomb walls. While the Temple stood the menorah was probably a symbol of the Temple and its rituals. In the period after the destruction of the Jerusalem Temple, the menorah became the most popular symbol of the Jewish religion.

Fig. 6.   Bronze plaque, possibly from a synagogue, depicting menorah with lulav (palm branch) on left and shofar (ram's horn) on right, circa 3rd – 5th centuries CE, found in Israel.
Courtesy private collection.

Fig. 7.   Bronze amulet depicting menorah, with lulav (palm branch) to left and shofar (ram's horn) to right; a typical rosette motif appears on the other side, circa 3rd – 5th centuries CE, found in Israel.
Courtesy private collection.

Fig. 8.   Roman Period carnelian seal depicting menorah flanked by two bunches of grapes, 2nd – 3rd centuries CE.
ANS Collection 0000.999.36807. Newell bequest.

Fig. 9.   The menorah flanked
by olive branches is the official
symbol of the State of Israel.
Photograph: Aaron Hendin.

Fig. 10. Chanukah menorah, c.
mid-20th century, Israel.
Courtesy private collection.

A bronze menorah (Fig. 9), patterned after the one shown on the
Arch of Titus, stands across from the Knesset (Parliament) in Jerusalem. It was a gift of the British Government on the eighth anniversary
of the founding of the State of Israel. It has 29 various motifs with
figures that depict different periods in Jewish history. The menorah re-
inforces the idea that Israel should be "a light unto the nations" (Isaiah
42:6).

The nine-branched menorah used on the festival of Chanukah, is
traditionally patterned after the Temple menorah, because Chanukah
celebrates the miracle that a day's worth of oil, purified for sacred use,
lasted for eight days. Most modern menorahs (see Fig. 10) are made to
burn wax candles, but in earlier times they burned olive oil.

> In the year 170 (142 BCE) Israel was released from the gen-
> tile yoke. The people began to write on their contracts and
> agreements, 'in the first year of Simon, the great high priest,
> general and leader of the Jews' – I MACCABEES 13: 41-42.

Simon was brother of Judah Maccabee, whose victory against Antiochus IV in 166 BCE, is retold every year during the holiday of Chanukah. Simon never struck coins, but his son, John Hyrcanus I (134 – 104 BCE) and other descendants continued to strike coins until Herod the Great became ruler of Judaea.

Hyrcanus I's title was "High Priest," and his son Alexander Jannaeus (104 – 76 BCE) was the first Jewish ruler to be named both "King" and "High Priest" on his coins. Jannaeus also added the anchor to his coins to commemorate his rule over port cities, and also the star and diadem, which signified royalty.

HERODIANS AND THE JUDEO-CHRISTIAN TRADITION

Coins of Herod I (the Great)

Herod's father, Antipater, was chief advisor to the later Maccabean kings. In 40 BCE Herod was declared king by the Roman senate.

It took Herod and his Roman allies three years to capture Jerusalem. Herod ruled Judaea by the grace of Rome. His administration was Hellenistic in character, and since he was not from a priestly family he had to appoint High Priests for the Temple, which he did for political or financial gain instead of tradition and Jewish law.

Herod was paranoid about his position over the Jews. He sentenced his beloved wife, Mariamne, and two of his sons to death because they were from the popular Maccabean family and he believed they might be political threats. When the emperor Augustus heard about these murders, he reportedly said, "It is better to be Herod's pig than his son" ironically referring to the fact that as a Jew, Herod did not eat pork.

Herod embarked on many construction and cultural projects to advance his policies and reputation. He built the best port in the ancient world at Caesarea Maritima, and fortresses, palaces, and theatres, both inside and far removed from his territories.

Herod hoped to improve his status with the Jewish people by re-
storing the Jerusalem Temple, and he made it the most magnificent
Temple in the world. Herod did not offend his fellow Jews by bringing
statues or other effigies into Jerusalem until late in his reign, when he
affixed a golden eagle to the Temple gate. The people of Jerusalem
promptly tore it down. Herod was king when Jesus was born.

21   22

21. Herod I (40 – 4 BCE) bronze 8 prutot, struck 37 BCE.
     Obverse: Military helmet, frontal view, wreath featuring acan-
         thus leaf around, cheek pieces and straps, star above flanked by
         palm branches.
     Reverse: ΗΡΩΔΟΥ ΒΑΣΙΛΕΩΣ (*of King Herod*); tripod, ceremo-
         nial bowl (lebes) above, flanked by date ΛΓ (*year 3*) and mono-
         gram Ᵽ.
     Courtesy The Abraham D. Sofaer Collection on loan at the ANS.

22. Herod I bronze 2 prutot.
     Obverse: ΗΡΩΔΟΥ ΒΑCΙΛΕΩC (*of King Herod*); cross within
         closed diadem.
     Reverse: Tripod table, flat object (vessel?) upon it, flanked by
         palm branches.
     Courtesy The Abraham D. Sofaer Collection on loan at the ANS.
     The table is similar to tripod tables found in excavations near the Jerusa-
     lem Temple (see Fig. 11).

Fig. 11. Tripod table reconstructed from
ruins from the excavations near the Jerusalem Temple. Image: Meshorer, A Treasury of
Jewish Coins.

Fig. 12. The Western Wall (also called the Wailing Wall). After the destruction of the Temple in 70 CE this wall, which was part of the retaining wall built by Herod to support the great earthen platform upon which the Temple stood became a holy site to Jews. Photograph ANS Collection, by Felix Bonfils, mid 19th century CE.

23   24

23. Herod I bronze prutah.
    Obverse: HPW BACIΛ (*of King Herod*);   anchor.
    Reverse: Double cornucopia with caduceus between, dots
       above.
    Courtesy The Abraham D. Sofaer Collection on loan at the ANS.
    This coin may have been struck by Herod to commemorate the construction of his magnificent harbor at Caesarea Maritima.

24. Herod I bronze half-prutah.
    Obverse: BACIΛ HPWΔ (*of King Herod*); cornucopia with inscription above and below.
    Reverse: Eagle standing r.
    Courtesy The Abraham D. Sofaer Collection on loan at the ANS.
    This may represent the golden eagle Herod placed above the Temple gate late in his reign. It is the first image of a living creature to appear on a coin struck by a Jewish king.

25   26

25. Herod I bronze prutah.
     Obverse: HPΩΔOY BACIΛEΩC (*of King Herod*); around open
     diadem, inscription often incomplete.
     Reverse: Tripod table.
     Courtesy The Abraham D. Sofaer Collection on loan at the ANS.

26. Herod I bronze half-prutah.
     Obverse: HPΩΔOY BACIΛEΩC (*of King Herod*) in uneven lines.
     Reverse: Anchor within circle decorated with stylized lily flow-
     ers.
     Courtesy The Abraham D. Sofaer Collection on loan at the ANS.

SONS OF HEROD

When Herod I died in 4 BCE his kingdom was divided among his sons
Antipas, who became tetrarch of Galilee; Archelaus, who became ethnarch of Judaea; and Philip, who became tetrarch of Ituraea and Tra-
chonitas in the northeast.

Herod Archelaus

The tyranny and excesses of Archelaus (4 BCE – 6 CE) were so offen-
sive that in the ninth year of his reign, his subjects sent a delegation
to Rome to complain to Augustus. He was thus banished to Vienna in
Gaul.

> But when he heard that Archelaus did reign in Judaea in
> the room of his father Herod, he was afraid to go thither —
> MATTHEW 2:22.

27. Herod Archelaus (4 BCE – 6 CE) bronze two-prutot.
     Obverse: HPWΔHC (*Herod*); double cornucopias, adorned with
       grapes, horns parallel, turned to the l.
     Reverse: EΘN PXA CH (*Ethnarch*); war galley facing left with
       aphlaston, oars, cabin, ram.
     Courtesy The Abraham D. Sofaer Collection on loan at the ANS.

27   28

28. Herod Archelaus bronze prutah.
   Obverse: EΘNAPXOY (*of the Ethnarch*); crested helmet with cheek straps, viewed from front, caduceus below l.
   Reverse: HPWΔOY (*of Herod*); bunch of grapes on vine with small leaf on left.
   Courtesy The Abraham D. Sofaer Collection on loan at the ANS.

29

29. Herod Archelaus bronze half-prutah.
   Obverse: HPW (*of Herod*); prow of galley facing l.
   Reverse: EΘN (*of the Ethnarch*) within wreath.
   Courtesy The Abraham D. Sofaer Collection on loan at the ANS.

Herod Antipas

Herod Antipas (4 BCE – 37 CE) was referred to by Jesus as "that fox" (Luke 13: 32). Antipas is the "Herod" mentioned most frequently in the New Testament. He ordered the execution of John the Baptist. Pontius Pilate sent Jesus to Antipas when he learned he was a Galilean. When Caligula became emperor in 37 CE, Agrippa I, a grandson of Herod the Great, gained favor in Rome. He plotted to make his uncle Antipas appear to be a traitor, and succeeded. Caligula banished Antipas to Lugdunum in Gaul and confiscated his property, adding it to Agrippa's kingdom.

30   31

30. Herod Antipas (4 BCE – 37 CE) bronze full-denomination, struck
     19/20 CE at Tiberias.
     Obverse: TIBE PIAC (*Tiberias*) within wreath.
     Reverse: HPWΔOY TETPAPXOY (*of Herod the Tetrarch*); L KΔ
     (*year 24*) in fields; reed upright.
     Courtesy The Abraham D. Sofaer Collection on loan at the ANS.

31. Herod Antipas bronze half-denomination, struck 19/20 CE at
     Tiberias.
     Obverse: TIBE PIAC (*Tiberias*) within wreath.
     Reverse: HPWΔOY TETPAPXOY (*of Herod the Tetrarch*); L KΔ
     (*year 24*) in fields; reed upright.
     Courtesy The Abraham D. Sofaer Collection on loan at the ANS.

32   33

32. Herod Antipas bronze full-denomination, struck 29/30 CE at
     Tiberias.
     Obverse: TIBE PIAC within wreath.
     Reverse: HPWΔOY TETPAPXOY; L ΛΓ (*year 33*) in fields; palm
       branch upright.
     Courtesy The Abraham D. Sofaer Collection on loan at the ANS.

33. Herod Antipas bronze full denomination, struck 39/40 CE at
     Tiberias.
     Obverse: ΓΑΙΩ ΚΑΙCΑΡ ΓΕΡΜΑ ΝΙΚΩ (*for Gaius Caesar Ger-
     manicus*) within wreath.
     Reverse: HPWΔHC TETPAPXHC (*Herod the Tetrarch*); ETOC
     ΜΓ (*year 43* = 39/40 CE) in fields; seven-branched palm tree
     with two date clusters.
     Courtesy The Abraham D. Sofaer Collection on loan at the ANS.

34

Herod Philip

Philip (4 BCE – 34 CE) was the first Jewish king who violated Mosaic Law regarding graven images by having his own portrait, as well as portraits of Augustus and Tiberius, placed upon his coins. He was the first husband of the notorious Salome (see no. 41), his niece. Philip was generally a peace-loving man and a good administrator of his territories. On his death in 34 CE he was buried at Bethsaida.

> Now in the 15th year of the reign of Tiberius Caesar, Pontius Pilate being governor of Judaea and Herod being tetrarch of Galilee, and his brother Philip tetrarch of Ituraea and of the region of Trachonitis – LUKE 3: 1.

34. Herod Philip (4 BCE – 37 A.D) bronze, struck 1/2 CE at Paneas.
    Obverse: **KAICAP CEBACTOY** (*of Caesar Augustus*); bare head of Augustus to r.
    Reverse: **ΦΙΛΙΠΠΟΥ ΤΕΤΡΑΡΧΟΥ** (*of Philip the Tetrarch*); **LE** (*year 5* = 1/2 CE) in fields; bare head of Herod Philip r.
    Courtesy The Abraham D. Sofaer Collection on loan at the ANS.

35   36

35. Herod Philip bronze, struck 15/16 CE at Paneas.
    Obverse: **TIB KAICAPI ΣEBAΣ** (*for Tib[erius] Caesar Augustus*); laureate head of Tiberius to r.
    Reverse: **ΦΙΛΙΠΟΥ ΤΕΤΡΑΧΟΥ; L IΘ** (*year 19* = 15/16 CE) between columns of the Augusteum of Paneas, no podium, staircase below, dot in pediment.
    Courtesy The Abraham D. Sofaer Collection on loan at the ANS.

36. Herod Philip, struck 30/31 BCE at Paneas.
    Obverse: **ΦΙΛΙΠΠΟΥ** (*of Philip*); bare head of Herod Philip to r.
    Reverse: **L Λ Δ** (*year 34* = 30/31 CE) within wreath.
    Courtesy The Abraham D. Sofaer Collection on loan at the ANS.

Agrippa I, The King who Killed James

Agrippa I (37 – 44 CE) was well acquainted with the Herodian tradition of practical politics. He played a major role in helping Claudius to the throne when Caligula was killed. In gratitude, Claudius gave Agrippa the entire kingdom of his grandfather Herod the Great.

Many people know Agrippa best of all the Herodians because he was portrayed as Claudius' friend in the popular book and television drama *I Claudius* by Robert Graves.

Although Agrippa was a friend of Rome, he was also pro-Jewish and worked to fortify Jerusalem. Always the practical self-promoter, however, on some of coins he proclaims himself "King Agrippa, the Great Lover of Caesar." On Agrippa's orders, James son of Zebedee, one of the twelve apostles, was beheaded, and Peter was imprisoned (Acts 12;1-23).

> Now about that time Herod [Agrippa I] the king stretched forth his hands to vex certain of the church. And he killed James the brother of John with the sword – ACTS 12: 1-2.

37   38

37. Agrippa I (37 – 44 CE) bronze, struck 37/38 CE at Paneas.
     Obverse: BACIΛEΩC AΓPIΠΠAC (*of King Agrippa*); diademed head of Agrippa I to r.
     Reverse: AΓPIΠΠA YIOY BACIΛEΩC (*Agrippa, son of the king*); Agrippa II rides horse r., LB (*year 2* = 37/38 CE) beneath horse.
     Courtesy The Abraham D. Sofaer Collection on loan at the ANS.

38. Agrippa I bronze prutah, struck 41/42 CE at Jerusalem.
    Obverse: BACIΛEWC AΓPIΠA (*of King Agrippa*); umbrella-like canopy with fringes.
    Reverse: Lϛ (*year 6* = 41/42 CE) flanks three ears of barley and leaves.
    Courtesy The Abraham D. Sofaer Collection on loan at the ANS.

Herod, King of Chalcis

The descendants of Herod I remained loyal to Rome, and thus received both rank and privilege. This enabled them to rule not only Jewish districts, but also large areas in the Near East that had little or no connection with the Jews. Herod of Chalcis (41 – 48 CE) was Agrippa I's brother, and ruled over a territory in Coele-Syria to the north. Aristobulus (54 – 92 CE) became king of Armenia Minor. Among Herod the Great's other descendants were a grandson Tigranes V (6 – 12 CE) and Tigranes VI (60 – 62 CE) who became kings of Armenia.

39

39. Herod King of Chalcis bronze, struck 43/44 CE.
    Obverse: ΒΑΣΙΛΕΥΣ ΗΡΩΔΗΣ ΦΙΛΟΚΛΑΥΔΙΟΣ (*King Herod, friend of Claudius*); diademed bust of Herod of Chalcis to r.
    Reverse: ΚΛΑΥΔΙΩ ΚΑΙΣΑΡΙ ΣΕΒΑΣΤΩ ΕΤ Γ (*for Claudius Caesar Augustus, year 3* = 43/44 CE); within a circle and wreath.
    Courtesy The Abraham D. Sofaer Collection on loan at the ANS.

Aristobulus King of Armenia Minor & Queen Salome

Salute Apelles approved in Christ. Salute them which are of
Aristobulus' household — ROMANS 16: 10.

Salome was the dancing daughter of Herodias and she is the one who
asked Herod Antipas for John's head on a charger (platter). Later in life
after the death of her first husband Herod Philip, she married another
Herodian descendant, Aristobulus, King of Armenia. This coin is one
of fewer than a dozen known examples with her portrait, one of the
few lifetime portraits of any person mentioned in the New Testament.

> And when the daughter of the said Herodias came in and
> danced, and pleased Herod...the king said unto the dam-
> sel, ask me whatsoever thou wilt... And she came in...and
> asked, saying, I will that thou give me by and by in a charger
> the head of John the Baptist – MARK 6: 22-25.

40   41

40. Aristobulus, King of Armenia (54-92 CE) bronze, struck 56/57
CE.
Obverse: ΒΑCΙΛΕΩC ΑΡΙCΤΟΒΟΥΛΟΥ ΕΤ Γ (*of King Aristobu-
lus, year 3* = 56/57 CE); diademed bust of Aristobulus to l.
Reverse: ΒΑCΙΛΙCCΗC CΑΛΩΜΗC (*of Queen Salome*); bust of
Salome to l.
Courtesy The Abraham D. Sofaer Collection on loan at the ANS.

41. Aristobulus King of Armenia bronze, struck 66/67 CE.
Obverse: ΒΑCΙΛΕΩC ΑΡΙCΤΟΒΟΥΛΟΥ ΕΤ ΙΓ (*of King Aristobu-
lus, year 8* = 67/68 CE); diademed bust of Aristobulus to l.
Reverse: ΝΕΡΩΝΙ ΚΛΑΥΔΙΩ ΚΑΙCΑΡΙ CΕΒΑCΤΩ
ΓΕΡΜΑΝΙΚΩ (*for Nero Claudius Caesar Augustus Germanicus*)
within a wreath.
Courtesy The Abraham D. Sofaer Collection on loan at the ANS.

Agrippa II, Paul Almost Persuaded Him

When his father died in 44 CE, Agrippa II was only 17 years old. Claudius wanted to give him at least part of the kingdom of Agrippa I, but advisors argued that he was too young. So, Claudius again brought the Jewish kingdom under the direct rule of Rome and sent Procurator Cuspius Fadius to govern.

When Herod, king of Chalcis died in 48 CE, Claudius gave his throne to Agrippa II. Agrippa's kingdom was expanded under Nero, Vespasian, and his successors. The one area that never fell under Agrippa II's rule was Judaea, which was still governed by procurators of Rome. However, Agrippa II was given the right to oversee the affairs of the Jerusalem Temple, and to appoint the High Priest. Agrippa II was known as a weak leader, but still, he ruled for nearly 50 years because of his loyalty to Rome, especially during the Jewish War of 66 – 70 CE.

> King Agrippa, do you believe in prophets? I know that you do. And Agrippa replied to Paul, In a short time you will persuade me to become a Christian – ACTS 26: 27-28.

42

42. Agrippa II (55/56 – 95/96 CE) bronze, struck 75/76 CE at Paneas.

Obverse: ΑΥΤΟΚΡΑ ΚΑΙCΑΡ ΤΙΤΟC ΚΑΙ ΔΟΜΙΤΙΑΝΟC (*Emperors Caesar Titus and Domitian*); confronted laureate busts of Titus on l. and Domitian on r.

Reverse: ΒΑCΙΛΕΩC ΑΓΡΙΠΠΑ ΕΤΟΥC ΚΖ (*of King Agrippa, year 27 = 75/76 CE*); Pan walks l., playing pipes (*syrinx*) held in r. hand and holds *pedum* over l. shoulder, tree trunk on r., small crescent in upper l. field.

Courtesy The Abraham D. Sofaer Collection on loan at the ANS.

43

43. Agrippa II bronze medallion, struck 75/76 CE, struck at Caesarea Paneas.

Obverse: ΑΥΤΟΚΡΑ ΟΥΕCΠΑCΙΑΝΩ ΚΑΙCΑΡΙ CΕΒΑCΤΩ (*for Emperor Vespasian Caesar Augustus*); laureate, slightly draped bust of Vespasian to r.

Reverse: ΒΑCΙΛΕΩC ΑΓΡΙΠΠΑ–ΕΤΟΥC ΚΖ (*of King Agrippa, year 27 = 75/76 CE*); Pan walks l., playing pipes (syrinx) held in r. hand and holds pedum over l. shoulder, tree trunk on r., small crescent in upper l. field.

Courtesy The Abraham D. Sofaer Collection on loan at the ANS.

44

44. Agrippa II large bronze, struck 75/76 CE at Caesarea Paneas.

Obverse: ΑΥΤΟΚΡΑ ΟΥΕCΠΑCΙ ΚΑΙCΑΡ CΕΒΑCΤΩ (*for Emperor Vespasian Caesar Augustus*); laureate bust of Vespasian to r.

Reverse: ΕΤΟΥ ΚΖ ΒΑ ΑΓΡΙΠΠΑ (*year 27, King Agrippa = 75/76 CE*) across fields; Tyche-Demeter stands l. wearing kalathos, holding grain ears in r. hand and cornucopia in l., star in field l.

Courtesy The Abraham D. Sofaer Collection on loan at the ANS.

Roman Prefects and Procurators

The prefects and procurators (Roman governors) imposed stiff taxes and harsh rules on the people of Judaea. Pontius Pilate caused special strains on the relations between Rome and the Jews. Pilate is probably the most infamous of them because of his role in the trial of Jesus.

Many of the procurators were excessively cruel. Of the last procurator, Gessius Florus, Josephus wrote that "he made an open boast of his crimes against the people; he practiced every sort of robbery and abuse precisely as though he had been sent to punish condemned criminals..." Under Florus' rule, the Jews ceased their daily sacrifice for the emperor, and thus war with Rome was declared.

The prefects and procurators of Judaea did not put their own names on the coins struck during their rule. Instead they used the names of their patron emperors or other royal family members. Coins of Coponius and Ambibulus, prefects under Augustus, carry the name "Caesar." Coins of Valerius Gratus and Pontius Pilate, prefects under Tiberius, carry the names "Tiberius," "Tiberius Caesar" and Caesar, as well as "Julia" referring to Julia Livia, mother of Tiberius. Antoninus Felix, procurator under Claudius, carries more names than any of the other procurators: "Julia Agrippina," the wife of Claudius; "Tiberius Claudius Caesar Germanicus," royal name of Claudius himself; "Nero Claudius Caesar," son of Claudius; and "Brittanicus," younger son of Claudius. The single coin type of Porcius Festus, procurator under Nero, carries only the name of Nero and the title "Caesar."

Coponius

45

45. Under Augustus (27 BCE – 14 CE). Coponius (5 – 8 CE) bronze prutah, struck 5/6 CE.
     Obverse: KAICAPOC (*of Caesar*); ear of grain curved to right.
     Reverse: Eight-branched palm tree bearing two bunches of dates; LΛϚ (*year 36 = 5/6 CE*).
     Courtesy The Abraham D. Sofaer Collection on loan at the ANS.

Pontius Pilate

> And when they had bound him, they led him away, and delivered him to Pontius Pilate the governor – MATTHEW 27: 2.

45   46

45. Under Tiberius (14 – 37 CE). Pontius Pilate (26 – 36 CE) bronze prutah, struck 29/30 CE.

Obverse: ΙΟΥΛΙΑ ΚΑΙCΑΡΟC (*Julia the Queen*); three bound ears of grain, the outer two droop.

Reverse: ΤΙΒΕΡΙΟΥ ΚΑΙCΑΡΟC LIϚ (*of Tiberius Caesar, year 16 = 29/30 CE*); libation ladle (simpulum).

Courtesy The Abraham D. Sofaer Collection on loan at the ANS.

46. Under Tiberius. Pontius Pilate bronze prutah, struck 30/31 CE.

Obverse: LIZ (*year 17 = 30/31 CE*) within wreath.

Reverse: ΤΙΒΕΡΙΟΥ ΚΑΙCΑΡΟC (*of Tiberius Caesar*); lituus (augur's wand).

Courtesy The Abraham D. Sofaer Collection on loan at the ANS.

Fig. 13. Stone with Pontius Pilate inscription found at Caesarea, with Latin inscription that mentions the "Tiberium" a building built by "Pontius Pilate the prefect of Judaea." Israel Museum. Photograph: Meshorer, TestiMoney.

Antoninus Felix

And after certain days, when Felix came with his wife Drusilla, which was a Jewess, he sent for Paul, and heard him concerning the faith in Christ – Acts 24: 24

47   48   49

47. Under Claudius (41 – 54 CE). Antonius Felix (52 – 58 CE) bronze prutah, struck 54 CE.

    Obverse: NEPW KΛAY KAICAP (*Nero Clau[dius] Caesar*—son of Claudius); two oblong shields and spears crossed.

    Reverse: BPIT (*Brit[annicus]*—younger son of Claudius) above; LIΔ KAI (*year 14 of Caesar* = 54 CE) in fields; six-branched palm tree bearing two bunches of dates.

    Courtesy The Abraham D. Sofaer Collection on loan at the ANS.

48. Under Claudius. Antonius Felix bronze prutah, struck 54 CE.

    Obverse: IOY ΛIA AΓ PIΠΠI NA (*Julia Agrippina*—wife of Claudius) within wreath tied at bottom with an X.

    Reverse: TI KΛAYΔIOC KAICAP ΓEPM (*Ti[berius] Claudius Caesar Germ[anicus]*); LIΔ (*year 14* = 54 CE) beneath two crossed palm branches.

    Courtesy The Abraham D. Sofaer Collection on loan at the ANS.

Porcius Festus

After two years had passed, Felix was succeeded by Porcius Festus – Acts 24: 27.

49. Under Nero (54 – 58 CE) Porcius Festus (58 62 CE), struck in 58/59 CE.

    Obverse: NEP / WNO / C (*of Nero*) within wreath, X at base.

    Reverse: LE KAICAPOC (*year 5 of Caesar* = 58/59 CE); palm branch.

    Courtesy The Abraham D. Sofaer Collection on loan at the ANS.

THE JEWISH WARS

The Jewish War 66 to 70/73 CE

Since the death of Agrippa I in 44 CE, there had been many clashes between Romans and Jews. The land seethed with rebellion. Agrippa II pleaded with the Jews not to go to war and warned "[you will] be devastated by the enemy if you rebel."

Initial Jewish victories sent shock waves throughout the Roman Empire. Nero sent his most distinguished general, Vespasian, to the Holy Land. With the Roman Legions he fought his way through the North and to Jerusalem and by 68 CE Vespasian had crushed the revolt except for Jerusalem and the mountain fortress Masada.

Nero died in 68 and civil wars rocked Rome. The legions in the east proclaimed Vespasian emperor, and he put his son Titus in charge of the siege of Jerusalem. Inside the city three factions of Jews battled each other while they held off the Romans. Titus' siege machines pounded the city and its walls with battering rams and huge stones.

On the ninth day of the Jewish month of Av in 70 CE, Titus' troops broke into Jerusalem and looted the Temple and burned it. Jewish rebels in Masada held out and were not defeated until 73 CE.

50   51

50. Jewish War silver shekel year 1, struck 66/67 CE at Jerusalem.
     Obverse: ᛚᚠᚨᛋᚼᛋ ᛚᚦᛋ (שקל ישראל, *shekel of Israel*); ᚠ (א, *[year] 1*) above ritual chalice with smooth, wide rim, pellet on either side, the base has pearled ends, circle of dots all around chalice and also outer legend.
     Reverse: ᛨᛋᚹᚦᚦ ᛃᛚᛋᛏᚦᚨᛋ (ירושלם קדשה, *Jerusalem [the] holy*); stem with three pomegranates, pearl at base, circle of dots all around.
     ANS Collection: 2010.69.1. Gift of Abraham and Marion Sofaer.

51. Jewish War silver half-shekel year 1 struck at Jerusalem.
Obverse: ⌐ (חצי השקל, *half of a shekel*); א [*year*] *1*)
above ritual chalice with smooth rim, pellet on either side, flat
base with pearled ends.
Reverse: (ירושלם קדשה, *Jerusalem [the] holy*);
staff with three pomegranate buds, round base.
ANS Collection: 2010.69.4. Gift of Abraham and Marion Sofaer.

52. Jewish War silver shekel year 2, struck 67/68 CE at Jerusalem.
Obverse: (שקל ישראל, *shekel of Israel*); (שב, *year
2*) above ritual chalice with pearled rim, the base is raised by
projections on ends.
Reverse: (ירושלם הקדשה, *Jerusalem the
holy*); staff with three pomegranate buds, round base.
ANS Collection: 2010.69.7. Gift of Abraham and Marion Sofaer.

53. Jewish War silver half-shekel year 2, struck at Jerusalem.
Obverse: (חצי השקל, *half of a shekel*); ritual chalice with pearled rim, the base is raised by projections on ends,
above chalice date (בש, *year 2*).
Reverse: (ירושלם הקדשה, *Jerusalem the
holy*); staff with three pomegranate buds, round base.
ANS Collection: 2010.69.9. Gift of Abraham and Marion Sofaer.

54. Jewish War bronze prutah year 2, struck at Jerusalem.
Obverse: (שנת שתים, *year two*); amphora with broad
rim and two handles.
Reverse: (חרת ציון, *the freedom of Zion*); vine leaf on
small branch with tendril.
ANS Collection: 2010.69.11. Gift of Abraham and Marion Sofaer.

55

56

55. Jewish War silver shekel year 3, struck 67/68 CE at Jerusalem.
Obverse: 𐤔𐤒𐤋 𐤉𐤔𐤓𐤀𐤋 (שקל ישראל, *shekel of Israel*); 𐤔𐤂 (שג, *year 3*) above ritual chalice with pearled rim, the base is raised by projections on ends.
Reverse: 𐤉𐤓𐤅𐤔𐤋𐤌 𐤄𐤒𐤃𐤔𐤄 (ירושלם הקדשה, *Jerusalem the holy*); staff with three pomegranate buds, round base.
ANS Collection: 2010.69.29. Gift of Abraham and Marion Sofaer.

56. Jewish War silver half-shekel year 3, struck at Jerusalem.
Obverse: 𐤇𐤑𐤉 𐤄𐤔𐤒𐤋 (חצי השקל, *half of a shekel*); 𐤔𐤂 (שג, *year 3*) above ritual chalice with pearled rim, the base is raised by projcctions on ends.
Reverse: 𐤉𐤓𐤅𐤔𐤋𐤌 𐤄𐤒𐤃𐤔𐤄 (ירושלם הקדשה, *Jerusalem the holy*); staff with three pomegranate buds, round base.
ANS Collection: 2010.69.30. Gift of Abraham and Marion Sofaer.

57

58

57. Jewish War silver shekel year 4, struck 68/69 CE at Jerusalem.
Obverse: 𐤔𐤒𐤋 𐤉𐤔𐤓𐤀𐤋 (שקל ישראל, *shekel of Israel*); 𐤔𐤃 (שד, *year 4*) above ritual chalice with pearled rim, the base is raised by projections on ends.
Reverse: 𐤉𐤓𐤅𐤔𐤋𐤌 𐤄𐤒𐤃𐤔𐤄 (ירושלם הקדשה, *Jerusalem the holy*); staff with three pomegranate buds, round base.
ANS Collection: 2010.69.37. Gift of Abraham and Marion Sofaer.

58. Jewish War silver half-shekel year 4, struck at Jerusalem.

Obverse: ⌐ᴚᎮ ⌐ᎮᴚᎮ (חצי השקל, *half of a shekel*); ᎮW (שד, *year 4*) above ritual chalice with pearled rim, the base is raised by projections on ends.

Reverse: ᴚWᎮᎮᴬᴚ ᴚᴬᴢᴢWᎮᎮᴚ (ירושלם הקדשה, *Jerusalem the holy*); staff with three pomegranate buds, round base.

ANS Collection: 2010.69.38. Gift of Abraham and Marion Sofaer.

59   60

59. Jewish War bronze half-shekel year 4, struck at Jerusalem.

Obverse: ⌐ᎮᴚᎮ ᴏᴚᎮᴬᎮ ×ᴢW (שנת ארבע חצי, *year four, half*); two lulav bunches flank an etrog (citron).

Reverse: ᴢᴢᴚᎮ ×ᴸᴲᴚᴸ (לגאלת ציון *to the redemption of Zion*); Seven-branched palm tree with two bunches of dates, flanked by baskets of dates.

ANS Collection: 2010.69.39. Gift of Abraham and Marion Sofaer.

60. Jewish War bronze quarter-shekel year 4, struck at Jerusalem.

Obverse: ᴏᴚᎮᎮ ᴏᎮᎮᴬᴠ ×ᴢW (שנת ארבע רביע, *year four–quarter*); two lulav bunches.

Reverse: ᴢᴢᴚᎮ ×ᴸᴲᴚᴸ (לגאלת ציון *to the redemption of Zion*); etrog.

ANS Collection: 2010.69.40. Gift of Abraham and Marion Sofaer.

61. Jewish War bronze eighth-shekel year 4 struck at Jerusalem.

Obverse: ᴏᎮᎮᴠ ×ᴢW (שנת ארבע, *year four*); lulav bunch flanked by an etrog on either side.

Reverse: ᴢᴢᴚᎮ ×ᴸᴲᴚᴸ (לגאלת ציון *to the redemption of Zion*); chalice with pearled rim.

ANS Collection: 2010.69.45. Gift of Abraham and Marion Sofaer.

61   62

62. Jewish War silver shekel year 5, struck 69/70 CE at Jerusalem.
    Obverse: ⵣҒⵗWⵣ ⵣҎW (שקל ישראל, *shekel of Israel*); ⵥW (שה, *year 5*) above ritual chalice with pearled rim, the base is raised by projections on ends.
    Reverse: ⵥWᵗ⁹Ҏⵥ ⵗ⁹ⵣWᵗ⁹ⵣ (ירושלם הקדשה, *Jerusalem the holy*); staff with three pomegranate buds, round base.
    Courtesy private collection.

Judaea Captured

After Titus destroyed the Temple, Jews were expelled from Jerusalem. Titus and his father Vespasian, now Emperor of Rome, issued a large series of coins, struck at Caesarea, commemorating the Roman victory over the Jews. In spite of their defeat, many Jews remained in the area, and also a Jewish Diaspora grew throughout the ancient world, bolstered by refugees from the Holy Land. They looked toward the day that their Temple would be rebuilt. Other large series of the "Judaea Capta" coins were issued in Rome and other Imperial mints.

63

63. Vespasian (69 – 79 CE) bronze.
   Obverse: ΑΥΤΟΚΡ ΟΥΕΣΠΑΣΙΑΝΟΥ (*of Emperor Vespasian*);
   laureate head of Vespasian to r.
   Reverse: ΙΟΥΔΑΙΑΣ ΕΑΛWΚΥΑΣ (*Judaea captured*); Nike stands
   r. with l. foot on helmet; she writes with r. hand on shield hanging from palm tree.
   Courtesy The Abraham D. Sofaer Collection on loan at the ANS.

64   65

64. Titus (79-81 CE) bronze.
   Obverse: ΑΥΤΟΚΡ ΤΙΤΟΣ ΚΑΙΣΑΡ (*Emperor Titus Caesar*); laureate head of Titus to r.
   Reverse: ΙΟΥΔΑΙΑΣ ΕΑΛWΚΥΑΣ; Nike stands r. with l. foot on
   helmet; she writes ΑΥΤ Τ ΚΑΙC with r. hand on shield hanging
   from palm tree.
   Courtesy The Abraham D. Sofaer Collection on loan at the ANS.

65. Titus (79-81 CE), bronze.
   Obverse: ΑΥΤΟΚΡ ΤΙΤΟΣ ΚΑΙΣΑΡ (*Emperor Titus Caesar*); laureate head of Titus to r.
   Reverse: ΙΟΥΔΑΙΑΣ ΕΑΛΩΚΥΙΑΣ (sometimes different forms
   of C, Σ and Ω, W); trophy, Judaea sits mourning l. below l.,
   her hands tied, shield to r. of trophy.
   Courtesy The Abraham D. Sofaer Collection on loan at the ANS.

Bar Kokhba Revolt 132 to 135 CE

From 115 to 117 CE the Jews outside of the Holy Land began a series of revolts known as the War of Quietus which spread from Mesopotamia to Cyrenaica, Cyprus, Mesopotamia, and Egypt and resulted in the killing of many Romans in areas with large Jewish populations. The rebellions were ended by Roman forces principally led by the general Lusius Quietus, hence the title of the conflict.

Hadrian (117 – 138 CE) enacted a series of laws that affected the Jews who lived in the Holy Land; he forbade circumcision and renamed Jerusalem as Aelia Capitolina. The Jewish people sought salvation and a Messiah who would bring them home. In 132 CE they began a revolt in the Holy Land. Its spiritual leader was Rabbi Akiba and the military leader was known as Simon Bar Kokhba. Rabbi Akiba initially supported Bar Kokhba as the Messiah.

Bar Kokhba's fervent followers literally went underground. They lived in caves and manmade underground complexes throughout Judaea, from which they tormented Roman troops, causing considerable hardship for the first half of the war. Saint Jerome wrote that Bar Kokhba was such a ferocious warrior that he appeared to be "spewing out flames" when he went to battle.

Bar Kokhba's troops were defeated in 135 CE in a battle at Beitar, near Bethlehem; thus a flicker of freedom was extinguished for the Jewish People.

66

66. Bar Kokhba Revolt (132 – 135 CE) silver sela year 1, struck 132/133 CE.

Obverse: ירושלם (ירושלם, *Jerusalem*) on three sides of facade of the Jerusalem Temple, ark or showbread table (?) seen from end in center of entrance.

Reverse: שנת אחת לגאלת ישראל (שנת אחת לגאלת ישראל, *year one of the redemption of Israel*); *lulav* bunch with *etrog* at left.

ANS Collection: 2010.76.1. Gift of Abraham and Marion Sofaer.

67. Bar Kokhba Revolt bronze year 1.
   Obverse: ⌐𝔏𝔄𝔘𝔦 𝔄𝔏𝔘𝔍 𝔍𝔄𝔬𝔘𝔘 (שמעון נשיא ישראל, *Simon,
   Prince of Israel*); within a wreath.
   Reverse: ⌐𝔏𝔄𝔘𝔦 𝔛⌐𝔏𝔄𝔦 𝔛𝔄𝔏 𝔛𝔍𝔘 (שנת אחת לגאלת ישראל,
   year one of the redemption of Israel); amphora with two handles.
   ANS Collection: 2010.76.3. Gift of Abraham and Marion Sofaer.

68. Bar Kokhba Revolt bronze year 1.
   Obverse: ⌐𝔏𝔄𝔘𝔦 𝔄𝔏𝔚𝔍 𝔍𝔄𝔬𝔘𝔘 (שמעון נשיא ישראל,, *Simon,
   Prince of Israel*); palm branch within a wreath.
   Reverse: ⌐𝔏𝔄𝔘𝔦 𝔛⌐𝔏𝔄𝔦 𝔛𝔄𝔏 𝔛𝔍𝔘 (שנת אחת לגאלת ישראל,
   year one of the redemption of Israel); wide lyre (*nevel* or *chelys*) of
   6 (sometimes 4 or 5) strings.
   ANS Collection: 2010.76.16. Gift of Abraham and Marion Sofaer.

69. Bar Kokhba Revolt silver sela year 2, struck 133/134 CE.
   Obverse: 𝔘⌐W⸱𝔄⌐ (ירושלם, *Jerusalem*) on three sides of facade of
   Jerusalem Temple, ark or showbread table (?) seen from end in
   center of entrance.
   Reverse: ⌐𝔏𝔄𝔘𝔦 𝔮𝔄⌐ 𝔍𝔘 (שב לחר ישראל, *year two of the free-
   dom of Israel*); *lulav* with *etrog* at l.
   ANS Collection: 2010.76.30. Gift of Abraham and Marion Sofaer.

70. Bar Kokhba Revolt silver zuz year 2.

Obverse: ○ שׁ (מש ע, *Sm'*— abbreviating *Simon*), the letters form a triangle, in a wreath of thin branches wrapped around eight almonds, medallion at top, tendrils at bottom.

Reverse: שב לחר ישראל (*year two of the freedom of Israel*); wide lyre (*nevel* or *chelys*) with three strings, four dots on sound box.

ANS Collection: 2010.76.40. Gift of Abraham and Marion Sofaer

.

71

71. Bar Kokhba Revolt silver zuz year 2.

Obverse: שמעון (שמעון, *Simon*) in a wreath of thin branches wrapped around eight almonds, medallion at top, tendrils at bottom.

Reverse: שב לחר ישראל (שב לחר ישראל, *year two of the freedom of Israel*); two trumpets upright.

ANS Collection: 2010.76.137. Gift of Abraham and Marion Sofaer.

72

72. Bar Kokhba Revolt silver zuz year 2.

Obverse: שמעון (שמעון, *Simon*) bunch of grapes in three lobes hanging from branch, which has a leaf to the left and a tendril to the right.

Reverse: שב לחר ישראל (שב לחר ישראל, *year two of the freedom of Israel*); fluted jug, handle on l., willow branch on r.

ANS Collection: 2010.76.120. Gift of Abraham and Marion Sofaer.

73

73. Bar Kokhba Revolt silver sela undated, struck 134/135 CE.
Obverse: שמעון (שמעון, Simon) on two sides; wavy line above facade of the Jerusalem Temple, ark or showbread table (?) seen from end in center of entrance.
Reverse: לחרות ירושלם (לחרות ירושלם, for the freedom of Jerusalem); lulav with etrog at l.
ANS Collection: 2010.76.110. Gift of Abraham and Marion Sofaer.

74 75

74. Bar Kokhba Revolt silver zuz undated.
Obverse: שמעון (שמעון, *Simon*) in a wreath of thin branches wrapped around eight almonds, medallion at top, tendrils at bottom.
Reverse: לחרות ירושלם (לחרות ירושלם, *for the freedom of Jerusalem*); elongated lyre (*kinor* or *kithara*) with three strings.
ANS Collection: 2010.76.124. Gift of Abraham and Marion Sofaer.

75. Bar Kokhba Revolt bronze undated.
Obverse: שמעון (שמעון, *Simon*); seven-branched palm tree with two bunches of dates.
Reverse: לחרות ירושלם (לחרות ירושלם, *for the freedom of Jerusalem*); vine leaf on tendril.
ANS Collection: 2010.76.143. Gift of Abraham and Marion Sofaer.

76

76. Bar Kokhba Revolt bronze undated.
    Obverse: שמעון (שמעון, *Simon*) across fields; seven-branched palm tree with two bunches of dates.
    Reverse: לחרות ירושלם (לחרות ירושלם, *for the freedom of Jerusalem*); bunch of grapes with branch and small leaf.
    ANS Collection: 2010.76.168. Gift of Abraham and Marion Sofaer.

COINS THAT JESUS KNEW

There is no doubt that the coins of his time can help us to reconstruct better some portions of the world in which Jesus lived.

According to the Gospels, Jesus was well aware of the importance of money, whether coins or other forms of currency. During his lifetime, bronze coins of various denominations were manufactured in the Galilee, Judea, and Samaria, and many silver coins circulated in these areas even though none were manufactured there during this period. Both the bronze and silver coins were widely used. It follows that as a man who widely traveled in these lands, Jesus was familiar with the use of money, including coined money in both large and small transactions.

Since Jesus grew up in Nazareth, he surely knew the coins that circulated throughout the Galilee as well as those from Jerusalem and its environs. These included silver, bronze, and rarely gold, which may have been Judean, Greek, Roman, Syrian, and Nabataean coins. Some of the locally issued coins in wide circulation during the life of Jesus also included coins of the High Priests who were the nephews and great nephews of Judah Maccabee. Other circulating local coins included those of Herod the Great and his three sons Archelaus, who ruled in Judea, Antipas who ruled in Galilee, and Philip, who ruled in the farthest northern territories of the area.

The Temple Tribute

The coins struck at the city of Tyre in Phoenicia were known to be of pure silver and true weight. Every Jewish male over 20 years of age paid an annual Temple tax of a half-shekel (Exodus 30: 11-16). The Tyre coins were so trusted that this had to be paid in Tyre silver coins. The Talmud says that "Silver, whenever mentioned in the Pentateuch, is Tyrian Silver. What is Tyrian silver? It is a Jerusalemite."

It is ironic that the purity and weight of the Tyre coins caused them to be used at the Temple, even though they carried a graven image of the god Melqarth, who was a Tyrian version of Herakles. Coins, however, do not become "unclean vessels" when they are used in transactions.

77   78

77. Tyre, Phoenicia silver shekel, struck 14/15 CE.
    Obverse: Laureate head of Melqarth r., wears lion skin knotted around neck.
    Reverse: ΤΥΡΟΥ ΙΕΡΑΣ ΚΑΙ ΑΣΥΛΟΥ (*of Tyre the holy and inviolable*) Eagle standing l. with r. foot on prow of ship, palm branch over r. shoulder, date PM (*year 140*= 14/15 CE) and club are in field to l., a Phoenician letter between eagle's legs, in right field Greek letters KP, a monogram below.
    Courtesy The Abraham D. Sofaer Collection on loan at the ANS.

78. Tyre, Phoenicia. Silver half-shekel, struck 21/20 BCE.
    Obverse: Laureate head of Melqarth r., wears lion skin knotted around neck.
    Reverse: ΤΥΡΟΥ ΙΕΡΑΣ ΚΑΙ ΑΣΥΛΟΥ (*of Tyre the holy and inviolable*) Eagle standing l. with r. foot on prow of ship, palm branch over r. shoulder, Ρς (*year 106* = 21/20 BCE) and club are in field to l., a Phoenician letter between eagle's legs, in right field Greek letters KP, a monogram below.
    Courtesy The Abraham D. Sofaer Collection on loan at the ANS.

Thirty Pieces of Silver

> Then one of the 12, called Judas Iscariot, went unto the
> chief priests, and said unto them, What will ye give me, and
> I will deliver him unto you? And they covenanted with him
> for 30 pieces of silver – MATTHEW 26: 14-15.

Because of the prestige of the Tyre shekels and half shekels we can
assume that they were also the coins used in the infamous "30 pieces
of silver," the parable of the "coin in the fish's mouth" (Matthew 17:
24–27), and other biblical stories related to large silver coins.

The Kolbon Surcharge

Matthew does not mention an interesting side note, called the *kolbon*,
which was a kind of exchange fee that money changers would take for
converting money or breaking it into smaller change.

Financial transactions were governed by strict rules of the Temple
treasury. The Temple must receive best deal possible under all circum-
stances. Since money changers would have charged approximately 4%
of a shekel to break it into two half-shekels, there would be a surcharge
of 11 prutot. Thus if two donors paid with one shekel coin, they had
to pay the Temple two kolbon or around 11 prutah.

Some rabbis suggest that the "kolbon" was paid even when exact
change of a half-shekel was used. This is because the Temple treasury
would incur the same expense when re-converting the half shekels into
larger money.

The Ein Gedi Hoard Mystery

During a 1964 excavation at Ein Gedi on the shore of the Dead Sea,
archaeologists found remains of a house from the first century CE.

In a plaster wall they discovered a Herodian-style oil lamp containing 139 prutah coins, struck between the years of 6 and 66 CE in Jerusalem by the local Roman governors, called prefects or procurators, and
King Agrippa I. It was concluded that 139 small bronze coins could
not constitute a hoard in the usual sense, because their value was so
small.

Fig. 14. The Ein Gedi Hoard consisted of 139 prutahs in a Herodian period oil lamp and was hidden in a plaster wall in a home in Ein Gedi, near the Dead Sea, in 50 CE. (This is an exact reconstruction of the hoard composed of a genuine first century oil lamp and stone cover nearly identical to those found at Ein Gedi, and 139 ancient coins of the same kind found in the hoard.) Courtesy private collection..

The late Prof. Ya'akov Meshorer of The Israel Museum, Jerusalem, reconstructed the story: "A Jew in the year 60 CE built his house, and, while finishing it, before its last plaster stage, decided to hide a sacred amount of money in the wall to protect against the evil eye."

At this time the most sacred sum of money to the Jews was the half-shekel paid annually to the Temple. But, our first-century man did not want simply to put a single, silver half-shekel into his wall for luck, since a large number of coins might make a better impression. He also decided to put the coins into an oil lamp, a symbol of eternity.

But here is the mystery: a half-shekel was equal to only 128 prutah coins at this time. So why did the archaeologists find 139?

If the man had gone to a money changer to convert small change into a silver half-shekel, the only coin accepted at the Temple, a standard exchange fee would have equaled about 4% or 11 small bronzes. Adding 128 plus 11 is 139.

The owner of this house wanted to make sure that when it came to good luck for him and his family, every precaution was taken to ensure accuracy!

The Tribute Penny

> Is it lawful to give tribute to Caesar, or not? Shall we give,
> or shall we not give? But He, knowing their hypocrisy, said
> unto them, Why tempt ye me? Bring me a penny, that I may
> see it. And they brought it. And He saith unto them, Whose
> is this image and superscription? And they said unto Him,
> Caesar's. And Jesus, answering, said unto them, Render to
> Caesar the things that are Caesar's and to God the things
> that are God's – MARK 12: 14-17.

The denarius of Tiberius is most frequently considered to be the
coin referred to in this story. It could have been a coin of the previous emperor, Augustus, but the story took place during the reign of
Tiberius. His silver coins are scarce, but this is the most common type.

One may also ask why a "penny" was circulating at the time of
Jesus. It was a translation problem. In the 1611 edition of the King
James Bible, the word for denarius was translated as the Anglo-Saxon
penny, the standard silver denomination at the time.

79

79. Tiberius (14 – 37 CE) silver denarius.
    Obverse: TI CAESAR DIVI AVG F AVGVSTVS (*Tiberius, Caesar
    Augustus, Son of the Divine Augustus*); laureate bust of Tiberius r.
    Reverse: PONTIF MAXIM (*high priest*); female figure (Livia?) sits
    on a plain chair r., she holds olive branch in her l. hand and
    long scepter in her r.
    *The legend "high priest" refers to the Roman religion prior to its ac-
    ceptance of Christianity.*
    ANS Collection: 1935.117.357.

The Poor Widow's Mites

> And Jesus sat over against the treasury, and beheld how the people cast money into the treasury: and many that were rich cast in much. And there came a certain poor widow, and she threw in two mites, which make a farthing." – MARK 12: 41-44.

80. Alexander Jannaeus (103 – 76 BCE), bronze small prutahs (enlarged about 50%) with crude designs of anchors and stars, and mostly illegible legends. These may have been struck late in the reign of Jannaeus, or even by his wife and successor Salome Alexandra, or his brother Hyrcanus II, who reigned until 40 BCE. Apparently neither of those rulers issued coins in their own names.
Courtesy private collection.

Jesus was also familiar with the smallest financial instruments such as the poor widow's mites.

The poor widow's coins were small prutot, the smallest coins circulated in the ancient Holy Land at the time. Various sources say that one shekel was made up of between 256 and 768 prutahs. Thus, in any interpretation, the prutah was very small change indeed.

This parable probably originated during the late 20s CE Some may be surprised that these small bronze coins were still in circulation when they were struck by the Maccabean King Alexander Jannaeus around

78 BCE However, we know from archaeological evidence that small change was hard to come by in the ancient Holy Land and so Jannaeus' coins were used for up to 300 years.

Many people believe that the "mite" was the name of the smallest coin during the time of Jesus. That is not so. The word "mite" first appears in the 1525 English translation of Tyndale's New Testament.

Oliver Hoover, an Adjunct Curator at the American Numismatic Society, has studied coin-related words in the Bible. He explains that neither the original Greek of the New Testament nor the Latin Vulgate Bible, mentions the "mite." Instead the Greek or Latin words refer to either lepta or minuta respectively since there was no British parallel for any coin smaller than a farthing, which even in translation was double this tiny coin. Thus the English translators may have referred to the smaller denomination, the "mite" used by their Dutch trading partners in Flanders.

The word "mite" was disseminated by the King James Version, printed in 1611. It was among the most popular English versions of the Bible ever published.

As mentioned above, early English Bible translations reinterpreted the denominations of the Greek, Latin, and Hebrew scriptures in terms of sixteenth and seventeenth-century coins. The drachm or denarius became a silver "penny" after the British silver pennies of the day. Until Britain turned to a decimal currency system in 1971 the abbreviation for one penny remained "d" from the Latin denarius.

Parables about money allow us to understand that Jesus was well aware of the inherent value of the coins, and their usefulness in everyday life. Jesus was an astute observer and saw money as a symbol of human greed as well as a symbol of human goodness and charity.

CHRISTIANITY PORTRAYED ON COINS

For more than 1,000 years, the cross has been the most recognizable symbol of Christianity. But this was not always true. When Jesus was crucified in Jerusalem between 30 and 33 CE (the exact year is not known), he was one of many thousands of non-Romans who were dispatched by this ghastly form of capital punishment.

The cross did not become widely used as a symbol of Christianity until the late fourth century CE. The earliest Christian symbol used on coins was formed by the superimposed Greek letters chi (X) and rho (P) which looked like this ☧, and represented the first two letters of Christ in Greek (ΧΡΙΣΤΟΣ). This type of monogram as related to Christianity is also called a Christogram, and the Chi-Rho is one of the oldest examples. It first appeared on a coin of Constantine the Great (307 – 337 CE), who became the first Christian Emperor of Rome.

Constantine was with his army preparing for battle against his re-bellious co-Emperor Maxentius, on October 28, 312 CE at the Milvian Bridge outside of Rome. Eusebius, a contemporary historian, says Constantine told him that in the days before the battle, Constantine looked up at the sun and saw a cross of light above it with the Greek words 'Εν τούτωι νίκα, which translate into Latin as IN HOC SIGNO VINCES, or "In this sign, you will conquer." At first Constantine was not sure what it meant, but the next night he had a dream in which Jesus told him that he should use the sign against his enemies. The sign was described by another historian, Lactantius, who said it was a Latin cross with its upper end rounded like a P, so it had both the form of a cross and the monogram of Christ's name.

Constantine had this sign inscribed on helmets and shields of his soldiers, and he won the Battle of the Milvian Bridge and claimed the title Emperor. He believed his success was due to divine protection, and it influenced the course of history. In 313 CE. Constantine met his rival Licinius at Milan, where they issued the Edict of Milan, which allowed Christians to follow their faith.

In 325 CE, the Council of Nicea met and Constantine declared Christianity to be the Rome's official religion. It is not clear whether Constantine himself actually ever became a Christian. His mother, Helena, was not only converted but was so excited by her spiritual experience that it enticed her to make a pilgrimage, circa 326 CE, to Judaea, where she could visit all of the sites that were important in the life of Jesus.

81.   82

81. Constantine the Great (307 – 337 CE) bronze struck at Constantinople 327/328 CE.

Obverse: CONSTANTINVS MAX AVG (*Constantine the Great, Augustus*); laureate head r. of Constantine I.

Reverse: SPES PVBLIC (*hope for the public*); labarum with three medallions on drapery and crowned by Christogram, piercing serpent; in lower field r., A. In exergue, CONS.

Eusebius describes the labarum as a military standard made from a long pole with a gold spear used to form a cross, and on the top of it was "fixed a wreath of gold and precious stones; and within this, the symbol of the Savior's name…and these letters the emperor was in the habit of wearing on his helmet at a later period."
ANS Collection: 1886.11.1.

82. Vetranio (350 CE) bronze struck under Constantius II (337 – 361 CE) at Siscia.

Obverse: D N VETRANIO P F AVG / A; laureate, cuirassed and draped bust r. of Vetranio.

Reverse: HOC SIGNO VICTOR ERIS (*In this sign, you will conquer*); A in field, ASIS* in exergue; Emperor in military dress stands l., holding standard with Chi-Rho and spear; to r., Victory crowning Vetranio with a wreath and holding a palm branch.

The scene and legend on this coin provide a re-enactment of Constantine the Great's victory at the Milvian Bridge.
ANS Collection: 2010.33.1. Gift of Harlan J. Berk.

83. Constantine I as Augustus (307-337 CE) gold solidus
    Obverse: Diademed head of Constantine r., gazing upward.
    Reverse: VICTORIA CONSTANTINI AVG (*Victory of Constantine, Augustus*); Victory seated right on cuirass and shield, inscribing VOT / XXX on shield supported by Genius.
    In 313 CE Constantine met his rival Licinius at Milan, and they issued the Edict of Milan, which allowed Christians to follow their faith. This abolished penalties for practicing Christianity in the Roman Empire; confiscated churches and other Christian property were to be returned. Going forward, Constantine supported the Church, exempted clergymen from certain taxes, and promoted Christians to high office.
    ANS Collection: 1967.153.45.

84. Magnentius (350-353 CE) bronze coin.
    Obverse: Magnentius, bare-headed, draped bust r.
    Reverse: SALVS DD NN AVG ET CAES (*safety of our Lords the Augustus and the Caesar*) around a large Christogram dividing alpha and omega.
    ANS Collection: 1984.146.2203.

Fig. 15. Red terra cotta oil lamp decorated with Chi-Rho motif, North Africa, c. 4th – 5th centuries CE. Courtesy private collection.

Fig. 16. Church of the Holy Sepulchre, Jerusalem. Photograph ANS Collection by Felix Bonfils, mid 19th century CE.

One of Constantine's most famous building projects was the Church of the Holy Sepulchre in Jerusalem. Today's church is built upon Constantine's foundations. The Church stands within the Old City of Jerusalem at a site venerated as Golgotha, the Hill of Calvary, where Jesus was crucified and was also believed to contain the sepulchre where he was buried.

85

85. Theodosius (379 – 395 CE) bronze.
    Obverse: Laureate head of Theodosius r.
    Reverse: Cross in wreath.
    The labarum with the Chi-Rho soon evolved into another symbol, the cross, which, of course, corresponded to the cross upon which Jesus was crucified by the Romans on the hill of Golgotha in Jerusalem. Quickly, the cross became the pre-eminent symbol of Christianity. This was the first coin to feature the Christian Cross symbol.
    ANS Collection: 2010.34.1. Gift of David Hendin.

86   Tiberius II Constantine (578 – 582 CE) gold solidus, struck at
      Constantinople 579-582 CE.
      Obverse: dM TIb CONSTANT P P AVG (His royal name);
      crowned and cuirassed bust of Constantine facing, holding glo-
      bus cruciger and shield decorated with horseman-enemy motif.
      Reverse: VICTORIA AVGG (*Victory of the Emperors*) B, cross
      potent on four steps; in exergue, CONOB.
      ANS Collection: 1968.131.34.

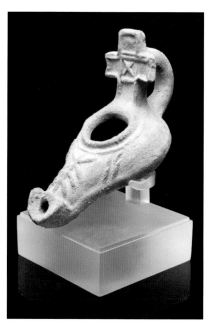

Fig. 17. Terra cotta oil lamp with cross for handle and 7-branched menorah
near spout, found Jerusalem area, c. 4th – 6th centuries CE. Private collection.

The cross and menorah are sometimes found together on oil lamps
of this period from the Holy Land, testifying to crossovers in early
Christianity and Judaism.

Fig. 18. Byzantine bronze crosses circa 8th – 10th centuries CE. Private collection.

Fig. 19. Via Dolorosa, Old City, Jerusalem and Fifth Station of the Cross Detail. Photographs: David Hendin.

The Via Dolorosa (Latin for "Way of Suffering") is said to be the path that Jesus walked carrying his cross. Along the way are fourteen stations, the first where Jesus was sentenced, and the last where he was laid in his tomb and covered with incense.

87

87.   Justinian II (First Reign 685-695 CE) gold solidus, Constantinople mint struck 692-695 CE.

Obverse: IhS CRISTOS REX RESNANTIUM (*Jesus Christ King of Kings*); facing bust of Christ, with long hair and full beard, wearing pallium and colobium, raising right hand in benediction, holding book of Gospels in left hand, cross behind head

Reverse: D IUSTINIANUS SERV ChRISTI (*Justinian, servant of Christ*); Justinian standing facing, wearing crown and loros, holding akakia and cross potent on base, CONOP in exergue.

Justinian II ascended to the throne when he was only 16. In the seventh year of his first reign, Justinian issued the first coin ever to bear the image of Jesus Christ. The coin may have been struck in 692 CE in response to the publication of Canon 82 of the Quinisext Council in Trullo, which decreed that all depictions of either God or Christ should be in human form, rather than that of the Paschal Lamb as previously required.

ANS Collection: 1980.109.279.

ARABS IN THE HOLY LAND

Nabataeans

The Nabataeans were ancient Arabs of the southern Levant and northern Arabia, who may be mentioned in Assyrian chronicles as early as the eighth century BCE. The Nabataeans were nomads, and their land had no defined borders. They inhabited a number of oases settlements, where they practiced advanced agriculture and became wealthy by controlling supplies of frankincense and bitumen. Matthew 2:11 notes that three gifts were given by magi on the birth of Jesus "...they presented unto him gifts; gold, and frankincense and myrrh." It is thus sometimes assumed that a Nabataean king or prince was one of the magi, but there is no confirmation in any sources.

Petra, the Nabataean capital, was described in John William Burgon's sonnet as the "rose red city half as old as time." Spectacular rock-hewn buildings and monuments were built in Hellenistic splendor in the first century BCE, when Petra had an estimated population of 20,000.

Fig. 20. The Rock Temple, Petra, photograph by Francis Frith (1822-1898).

88 89

88. Alexander the Great (336-323 BCE) gold stater.
Obverse: Helmeted head of Athena r.; thunderbolt below neck
Reverse: ΑΛΕΞΑΝΔΡΟΥ (*of Alexander*); Nike standing left, holding wreath and stylis.

Alexander planned to conquer the Nabataeans, but died before he had the chance. Alexander's successor Antigonus Monophthalmos sent a large Macedonian force, led by his son, against the Nabataeans in 312 BCE but failed to conquer them. The Nabataeans were skilled in desert guerilla warfare, and Petra was a nearly impregnable fortress.
ANS Collection: 1944.100.29740.

89. Proto-Nabataean bronze, c. 270 – 72 BCE.
Obverse: Helmeted head of Athena r.
Reverse: Winged Victory standing l., holding three branches in r. hand; in l. field crescent and Λ.

These are the earliest Nabataean coins and crudely copy the gold coins of Alexander the Great that the Nabataeans may have received in exhange for their expensive trade goods.
ANS Collection: 2010.55.10. Gift of David Hendin.

90 91

90. Aretas III (84-62 BCE) bronze showing the head of Aretas III. Struck in Damascus.
Obverse: Head of Aretas III r., diademed.
Reverse: Tyche of Damascus seated on rock l., holding cornucopia and extending hand; below, river god swimming; in three vertical lines: ΒΑΣΙΛΕΩΣ / ΑΡΕΤΟΥ / ΦΙΛΕΛΛΕΝΟΣ (*of King Aretas, Phihellene*); in l. field, ΑΡ.

ANS Collection: 2010.55.24. Gift of David Hendin.

Aretas III became king in 87 BCE. He extended his kingdom over what is now northern Jordan, southern Syria, and part of Saudia Arabia.

91. Roman Republic, M. Aemelius Scaurus and P. Plautius
    Hypsaeus, silver denarius struck 58 BCE.
    Obverse: M·SCAVR / AED CVR; King Aretas kneeling r., hold-
    ing olive branch and reins of camel standing beside him; on
    either side, EX – S·C.; in exergue, REX ARETAS.
    Reverse: P·HVPSAE / AED CVR; Jupiter in quadriga l. hold-
    ing reins in l. hand and hurling thunderbolt with r.; behind,
    CAPTV; below, C HVPSAE COS / PREIVE.
    ANS Collection: 1944.100.2590.

    *The Nabataeans were allies of the first Maccabees in their struggles
    against the Seleucid kings of Syria. But they soon became rivals of
    the Judaean dynasty. This conflict was a central reason that Pompey
    intervened in Judaea. Alexander Jannaeus forcibly converted many
    Nabataeans to Judaism.*

Hyrcanus II became king and High Priest of the Jews in 67 BCE and
shortly thereafter his younger brother Aristobulus II overthrew Hyrcanus and assumed his offices. Hyrcanus fled to Petra, where he allied
himself with Aretas III, who agreed to support him in exchange for
promises to return Arabian towns taken by the Maccabees.

With an army of 50,000, Aretas marched on Jerusalem and besieged
it for months. Aristobulus bribed Marcus Aemilius Scaurus, a lieuten-
ant of Pompey and governor of Syria, to aide him. Scaurus ordered
Aretas to withdraw and marched against him at his capital of Petra.

This coin commemorates the defeat of Aretas III by Scaurus. Aretas had to pay Scaurus 300 talents of silver to lift the siege of Petra.
Hyrcanus, ally of Aretas, was sent by Scaurus to the king to accept the
payment. Aretas thus retained his possessions, including Damascus,
and became a Roman vassal.

92.   93

92. Obodas II (62 – 60 BCE) silver drachm, struck 61 BCE.
    Obverse: Draped bust of Obodas II r., diademed.
    Reverse: Eagle standing l., Nabataean inscription:
    ברכת דושרא עבדת מלך נבטו) ודכת רז̇יפ6 שגרת כנ̇ כ̇ל̇ב̇ו̇9, *blessings of
    Dusares, Obodas king of the Nabataeans*); across field date: ש̇ נ̇ ת̇
    (שנת 2, *year 2 = 61 BCE*).
    Courtesy The Abraham D. Sofaer Collection on loan at the ANS.

93. Malichus I (60 – 30 BCE) bronze coin, struck 34 BCE.
    Obverse: Bust of Malichus I r., diademed with long curly hair.
    Reverse: Palm of hand with six fingers; ꝟꝟ Ɔ ꝟꝟ ꝟꝟ
    (מלכו מלכא מלך נבטו, *Malichus the king, king of the Nabataeans*);
    across field, date: IIIƷ ꝨꝞ (28 שנת, *year 28* = 34 BCE).

    Malichus I was son of Obodas. In 40 BCE he helped the Parthians over-
    run Syria and Palestine. After the Romans expelled the Parthians in
    34 BCE, they confiscated Malichus' date groves around Jericho and his
    harbors on the Red Sea. Herod I also defeated Malichus' army in 31
    BCE near Philadelphia (present-day Amman).
    Courtesy The Abraham D. Sofaer Collection on loan at the ANS.

94

94. Obodas III (30 – 9 BCE) silver drachm , struck 16 BCE.
    Obverse: Bust of Obodas III r., laureate; on r., ꝨꝞꝟ (עבדת, *Obo-*
    das).
    Reverse: Bust of the Nabataean queen r., veiled; on l., ꝟꝞꝟꝞ
    ꝨꝞꝟ (ברכת דושרא, *The blessing of Dousares*); on r., date: ꝟꝙ ꝨꝞ
    (15 שנת, *year 15* = 16 BCE).
    Courtesy The Abraham D. Sofaer Collection on loan at the ANS.

    Obodas III oversaw a cultural flowering during which most of the Naba-
    taean temples were built, including at Avdat, one of the famed cities of
    the Incense Route, the road over which valuable incense, perfumes, and
    spices were brought out of Arabia, across the Negev Desert, and to the
    Mediterranean ports. Avdat was named after him, and he was buried
    there. During the rule of Obodas, the Romans sought to discover the
    sources of the Nabataean perfume and spice trade.

95   96

95. Syllaeus (9 BCE), silver hemidrachm.
    Obverse: Head of Obodas III or Aretas IV r., diademed with
    long curly hair; in l. field Ƒ (ש, *S*).
    Reverse: Eagle standing l.; on r. and l., ꝉ Ƒ (חש, *S H*).
    Courtesy The Abraham D. Sofaer Collection on loan at the ANS.

Fig. 21.   Negev Desert seen via the ruins of Avdat. Photograph: A. Hendin.

Avdat was a camping ground and village for Nabataean caravans traveling along the Incense Route in the 3 – 2 centuries BCE.

96. Syllaeus, bronze.

Obverse: Bust of Syllaeus or Aretas IV r., laureate; on r. and l., H Ϝ (ח ש, S H).

Reverse: Double cornucopia crossed; on l., ϟϜ ligature of the name of Syllaeus: on r., H (ח, *H*).

ANS Collection: 2010.55.43. Gift of David Hendin.

Syllaeus was minister and advisor under king Obodas III and it appears that near the end of Obodas' reign Syllaeus unsuccessfully attempted to succeed him. Coins issued with his monogram appeared for only a brief period of time.

97. Aretas IV (9 BCE – 40 CE) and his first queen Huldu, silver drachm, struck 9 BCE.

Obverse: Bust of Aretas IV r., laureate; [...][...]

 חרתת מלך נבטו ,H‏תﬨ כﬨﬞﬞ ﬞﬞﬠﬞﬠ (חרתת מלך נבטו, Aretas, king of the Nabataeans).

Reverse: Draped bust of Huldu r., veiled; H﬩‏ כﬞﬞﬠﬞﬨ ﬞﬠﬞﬠﬞ‏ Ϝ﬩ﬨ I (חלדו מלכת נבטו שנת 1, *Huldu, queen of the Nabataeans, year 1 = 9* BCE).

Courtesy The Abraham D. Sofaer Collection on loan at the ANS.

97   98

98. Aretas IV and his second queen Shuqailait, bronze coin.
Obverse: Jugate busts of Aretas IV and Shuqailat r.; above, ﬥﬞﬞﬞ
(שלם, *whole*); in r. field, ﬥ (ש, *S*).
Reverse: Double cornucopia crossed; between horns, three-line
inscription: ﬥﬞﬞﬞ/ﬞﬞﬞ/ﬞﬞﬞﬞﬞ (חרתת שקילת, *Aretas, Shuqailat*).
ANS Collection: 2010.55.123. Gift of David Hendin.

*Aretas IV was the greatest Nabataean king. His daughter, Phasaelis,
married Herod Antipas, son of Herod I and tetrarch of Galilee. However, in 32 BCE, when Antipas divorced her to marry Herodias (mother
of Salome), Phasaelis returned to her father, who went to war against
Antipas and defeated him. Antipas appealed to Tiberius, who sent
troops to attack Aretas. In Corinthians 11: 32-33, the Apostle Paul tells
that he had to sneak out of Damascus in a basket through a window in
the wall to escape King Aretas.*

99   100

99. Malichus II (40 – 70 CE) and his sister Shuqailat II, silver
drachm, struck 40 CE.
Obverse: Draped bust of Malichus II r., laureate with long hair;
ﬥﬞﬞﬞ ﬥﬞﬞﬞ ﬥﬞﬞﬞ ﬥﬞﬞ (1) ﬥﬞﬞﬞ ﬥﬞﬞﬞ, מלכו מלכא מלך נבטו שנת, *Malichus the
king, king of the Nabataeans, year 1 = 40 CE*).
Reverse: Bust of Shuqailat II r., veiled; ﬥﬞﬞﬞ ﬥﬞﬞﬞ ﬥﬞﬞ ﬥﬞﬞﬞ
(שקילת אחתה מלכת נבטו), *Shuqailat his sister, queen of the Nabataeans*).
ANS Collection: 2010.55.166. Gift of David Hendin.

*Nabataean power began to wane during the reign of Malichus II, often
shown with his co-regent and sister Shuqailat II. The Romans had
succeeded in diverting the spice and perfume routes to Egypt. Malichus
had no choice but to cooperate with the greatest power in the ancient
world. In 66 CE when the Jewish War against Rome began, Malichus
sent 5,000 cavalry and 1,000 infantry to help Titus defeat the Jews.*

100. Rabbel II (70 – 105 BCE) and his mother Shuqailat, bronze coin.
Obverse: Jugate busts of Rabbell II and Shuqailat r.
Reverse: Double cornucopia crossed; between horns, ﬡﬞﬞﬞﬞﬞﬞ, ﬞﬞﬞﬞ
(שקילת, רבאל Rabbel, Shuqailat).
Courtesy The Abraham D. Sofaer Collection on loan at the ANS.

                 101   102

101. Rabbel II and his sister Gamilat, bronze coin.
Obverse: Jugate busts of Rabbel II and Gamilat r.
Reverse: Double cornucopia crossed; between, horns two-line
inscription: ﬞﬞﬞﬞ/ﬞﬞﬞﬞ (גמלת, רבאל, *Rabbel, Gamilat*).
Courtesy The Abraham D. Sofaer Collection on loan at the ANS.

102. Rabbel II and his sister Hagru, bronze coin.
Obverse: Jugate busts of Rabbel II and Hagru r.
Reverse: Double cornucopia crossed; between horns, two-line
inscription: ﬞﬞﬞ/ﬞﬞﬞﬞ (רבאל הגרו, *Rabbel, Hagru*).
ANS Collection: 2010.55.191. Gift of David Hendin.

Rabbel II was the last king of Nabataea. When his father Malichus II died he was still a child, and although he assumed the throne, his mother, Shuqailat, took control of the government and his sister, Gamilat, became queen. When Gamilat died, his sister Hagru became queen. When Rabbel II died, Trajan conquered the Nabataeans in 106, and their land became the Roman province of Arabia Petraea.

ISLAMIC COINS OF THE MIDDLE EAST

Umayyad Caliphate

The Umayyad Caliphate (in Arabic known as the *Banu Umayyah*, or *Sons of Umayyah*) was the second of the four major Arab caliphates established after the death of Muhammad in 632 CE (the first was the Rashidun). It was ruled by the dynasty, whose name derives from Umayya ibn Abd Shams, the great-grandfather of the first Umayyad caliph Uthman ibn Affan (644 – 656). At the time of its greatest power, the Umayyad Caliphate covered more than five million square miles. It was one of the largest empires the world had ever seen.

103   104

103. Arab Byzantine Iliya (Jerusalem), bronze fals under the Umayyads, 7th century CE.

    Obverse: Bearded figure of the caliph standing facing, wearing long robe, placing hand on his sword; Arabic inscription: لااله الا الله وحده (*there is no god but God alone*).

    Reverse: M, crescent below, Arabic inscription, upwards on l., ايليا (*Iliya*), upwards on r., فلسطين (*Filastin*).

    Courtesy The Abraham D. Sofaer Collection on loan at the ANS.

104. Arab Byzantine Tabariyya (Tiberias), bronze fals under the Umayyads, 7th century CE.

    Obverse: Three imperial figures standing facing.

    Reverse: M topped by monogram, ₽ and below A; Greek inscription starting on l., TIBEPIAΔOC; on r., Arabic inscription: طبرية (*Tabariyya*).

    Courtesy The Abraham D. Sofaer Collection on loan at the ANS.

    This coin copies a coin of Heraclius (610-641 CE).

105

105. Umayyad Akka (Akko) bronze fals, 7th century CE.

Obverse: Inscription in three lines surrounded by two dotted circles: لا اله / الا االله / وحده (*there is no god but God alone*).

Reverse: Inscription in three lines: محمد / رسول / االله (*Muhammad is the Messenger of God*); marginal inscription starting with five pointed star: بسم االله ضرب هذا الفلس بعكا (*in the name of God, this fals was struck at 'Akka*).

Courtesy The Abraham D. Sofaer Collection on loan at the ANS.

106   107

106. Umayyad Asqalan (Ascalon) bronze fals, 7th century CE.

Obverse: Inscription surrounded by three concentric dotted circles: لا اله الا / االله الا / لا شريك له (*there is no god but God, He has no associate*).

Reverse: Inscription in three lines: محمد / رسول / االله (*Muhammad is the Messenger of God*); marginal inscription: بسم االله ضرب هذا بعسقلن (*in the name of God, this was struck at Asqalan*), three stars are inlaid in the border of dots.

Courtesy The Abraham D. Sofaer Collection on loan at the ANS.

107. Umayyad Saffuriyya (Sepphoris) bronze fals, 7th century CE.

Obverse: Three line inscription in three concentric circles: لا اله / الا االله / وحده (*there is no god but God alone*).

Reverse: Three line inscription: محمد / رسول / االله (Muhammad is the Messenger of God); marginal inscription: بسم االله ضرب هذا الفلس بسفورية (*in the name of God, this fals was struck at Saffuriyya*).

Courtesy The Abraham D. Sofaer Collection on loan at the ANS.

Fig. 22.   The Dome of the Rock, Old City, Jerusalem. Photograph ANS Collection by Felix Bonfils, mid 19th century CE.

The Dome of the Rock in the Old City of Jerusalem was completed in 691 CE by orders of the Umayyad Caliph Abd al-Malik.

Fig. 23.   Hisham's Palace Mosaic, Jericho. Photograph by Aaron Hendin.

Hisham's Palace may have been the center of an Umayyad town, built by Al-Walid ibn Yazid around 743 – 744 CE during the caliphate of Hisham ibn Abd al-Malik. The central building was patterned after a Roman bath house, and contained fantastic mosaics and stucco motifs.

Abbasid Caliphate

The Abbasid caliphate was the third Islamic caliphate, and was founded by the descendants of Abbas ibn Abd al-Muttalib (566 – 662 CE),
one of the youngest uncles of Muhammad. During the Abbasid period
the Muslim world became the world's intellectual center for medicine,
science, and philosophy. Abbasids established the House of Wisdom
where both Muslim and non-Muslim scholars worked to gather and
translate all of the major written works into Arabic. The Abbasid caliphate encompassed the Golden Age of Islam, which flourished for
nearly 200 years.

108   109

108. Abbasid 'Akka (Akko) bronze fals, struck 815 CE.
     Obverse: Inscription in three lines:
     لا اله الا / االله / وحده / لا شريك له (*there is no god but God alone, He*
     has no associate); marginal inscription:
     ضرب هذا الفلس بعكا سنة مائتين (*this fals was struck at 'Akka in year*
     200 = 815 CE).
     Reverse: Inscription in three lines: محمد / رسول / االله
     (*Muhammad is the Messenger of God*); marginal inscription:
     با امر به الامير ابرهيم بن خمران (*as ordered by the Amir Ibrahim son*
     of Khumran).
     Courtesy The Abraham D. Sofaer Collection on loan at the ANS.

109. Abbasid Gaza bronze fals, struck 832 CE.
     Obverse: Inscription in three lines, in ornamented frame:
     لا اله الا / االله / وحده / لا شريك له (*there is no god but God, He has no*
     associate).
     Reverse: Inscription in four lines: محمد / رسول / االله / بخ
     (*Muhammad is the Messenger of God, good*); marginal
     inscription: ضرب هذا الفلس بغزة سنة سبع عشر و مائتين (*this fals was*
     struck at Gaza in the year 217 = 832 CE).
     Courtesy The Abraham D. Sofaer Collection on loan at the ANS.

Fig 24.   Al-Aqsa Mosque, Old City, Jerusalem. Photograph ANS Collection by Felix Bonfils, mid 19th century CE.

The al-Aqsa Mosque was originally a small prayer house, but the Umayyad caliph Abd al-Malik began to expand it, and it was finished by his son al-Walid in 705 CE. In 746 an earthquake completely destroyed it and it was rebuilt by the Abbasid caliph al-Mansur in 754 CE and again in 780 by his successor al-Mahdi. In 1033 another earthquake destroyed most of the structure, but within a few years the Fatimid caliph Ali az-Zahir build another mosque on the spot, and this is the building that remains today in Jerusalem.

Tulunids

The Tulunids (868 – 905 CE) were the first independent dynasty of Islamic Egypt. They broke away from the Abbasids and Ahmad ibn Tulun established his real authority. He and his successors reigned with nominal allegiance and Tulunid territory was expanded to Palestine, Syria, and small areas of Asia Minor.

110

110. Tulunid al-Ramlah gold dinar of Khumarawayh (884 – 896 CE), struck 892 CE.

Obverse: Inscription in three lines: لا اله الا / الله الا / لا شريك له / الله وحده
(*there is no god but God alone, He has no associate*); marginal inscription in two lines:

بسم الله ضرب هذا الدينر بفلسطين سنة تسع و سبعين و مائتين (*in the name of God, this dinar was struck at Filastin in the year 279* = 892 CE).

Reverse: Inscription in six lines:

الله / محمد / رسول / الله / المتمد على الله / خمارويه بن احمد (*to God, Muhammad is the Messenger of God, al-Mu'tamid 'ala Allah, Khumarawayh b. Ahmad*); marginal inscription:

محمد رسول الله ارسله بالهذى و دين الحق ليظهره على الدين كله لو كره المشركون (*Muhammad is the messenger of God, He has sent him with the guidance and the religion of truth so that he may proclaim it above every faith even if the polytheists dislike it*).

Courtesy The Abraham D. Sofaer Collection on loan at the ANS.

Ikhshidids

The Ikhshidid dynasty (935 – 969 CE) ruled as governors of Egypt and some related territories on behalf of the Abbasids. Muhammad bin Tughj Al-Ikhshid, a Turkic soldier, received his title *al-Ikhshid* (Soghdian for prince) from the Abbasid Caliph who appointed him. The dynasty came to an end when the Fatimid army conquered Cairo in 969.

111

111. Ikhshidid al Ramla gold dinar of Muhammad b. Tughj (935-946 CE), struck 943 CE.

Obverse: Inscription in five lines:

لا اله الا / الله وحده / لا شريك له / ابو منصور بن / امير المومنين (*there is no god but God alone, He has no associate, Abu Mansur son of the Commander of the Faithful*); inner marginal inscription:

بسم الله ضرب هذا الدينر بفلسطين سنة احدى و ثلثين وثلثمائة (*in the name of God, this dinar was struck at Filastin in the year 331 = 943* CE); outer marginal inscription:

الله الامر من قبل و من بعدو يومئذ يفرح المومنون بنصر الله (*to God* belongs the power before and after and in that day the believers shall rejoice in help of God).

Reverse: Inscription in six lines:

الله / محمد / رسول / الله / المتقى الله / الاخشيد (*to God, Muhammad is the Messenger of God, al-Muttaqi lillah, al-Ikhshid*); marginal inscription:

محمد رسول الله ارسله بالهذى و دين الحق ليظهره على الدين كله ولو كره المشركون (*Muhammad is the Messenger of God, He has sent him with the guidance and the religion of truth so that he may proclaim it above every faith even if the polytheists dislike it*).

Courtesy The Abraham D. Sofaer Collection on loan at the ANS.

Fatimids

The Fatimid Arab dynasty ruled over areas of North Africa, Egypt, the Levant, Sicily, and Yemen from 909 to 1171. The Fatimids claimed to be descendants of Fatima, the daughter of Muhammad, and wife of Ali, the fourth caliph. The Fatimids were said to have exercised a degree of religious tolerance towards non-Ismaili sects of Islam as well as towards Jews and Christians.

112

112. Fatimid Akka (Akko) gold dinar, struck 1090 CE.
   Obverse: Inscription in four lines:
   لا اله الا االله / و ١٦ م لا شريك له / محمد رسول، االله/ ولى االله (*there is no*
   god but God alone, He has no associate, 'Ali is the Friend of God);
   marginal inscription:
   محمد رسول االله ارسله بالهدى و دين الحق ليظهره على الدين كله و لو كره المشركون
   (*Muhammad is the Messenger of God, He has sent him with the*
   guidance and the religion of truth so that he may proclaim it above
   every faith, even if the idolaters dislike it).
   Reverse: Inscription in six lines:
   معد / عبد االله و وليه / الامام ابو تميم / المستنصر باالله / امير المؤمنين / عال
   (*Ma'ad, servant of God and His friend, the Imam Abu*
   Tamim, al-Mustansir billah, Commander of the Faithful;
   High [alloy]); marginal inscription:
   بسم االله الرحمن الرحيم ضرب هذا الذينر بعكا سنة ثلث و ثمانين و اربع مئة
   (*in the name of God, the Merciful, the Compassionate, this dinar*
   was struck at 'Akka in the year 483 = 1090 CE).
   Courtesy The Abraham D. Sofaer Collection on loan at the ANS.

COINS OF JERUSALEM

Jerusalem has been a city of importance since the earliest days of recorded history. Mints located in Jerusalem produced coins beginning during the Persian Period in the mid fourth century BCE. Many of the coins struck in this Holy City mention Jerusalem by name. Others illustrate symbols of the city, such as the lily. Still other coins show some of Jerusalem's most important buildings, including temples, churches, mosques, citadels, and gates. Some of these structures still exist today in modified form; others have been destroyed as each faith and ruling group tried to eliminate the previous cult center in order to establish its own.

Lily as Symbol of Jerusalem

> And they brought him upon horses, and buried him with his
> fathers in the city of Yehud (Judah) – II CHRONICLES 25: 28.

113   114

113. Yehud silver half-gerah, before 333 BCE.
     Obverse: Lily.
     Reverse: ᴟᴈ⅄ (*yhd*) above r. wing of falcon with wings spread, head r.
     Courtesy The Abraham D. Sofaer Collection on loan at the ANS.
     Yehud was not only the name of the Province of Judaea but also the name of the city of Jerusalem.

114. Hyrcanus I (134 – 104 BCE) in the name of Antiochus VII, struck 131/130 BCE.
     Obverse: Lily.
     Reverse: ΒΑΣΙΛΕΩΣ ΑΝΤΙΟΧΟΥ ΕΥΕΡΓΕΤΟΥ (*of King Antiochus, benefactor*); inverted anchor, below anchor ΒΠΡ (*year 181 = 131/130 BCE*).
     Courtesy The Abraham D. Sofaer Collection on loan at the ANS.

115

115. Alexander Jannaeus (104 – 76 BCE) bronze prutah.

Obverse: Lily flanked by paleo-Hebrew (יהונתן המלך, *Yehonatan the King*), border of dots.

Reverse: ΒΑΣΙΛΕΩΣ ΑΛΕΞΑΝΔΡΟΥ (*of King Alexander*); inverted anchor within circle.

Courtesy The Abraham D. Sofaer Collection on loan at the ANS.

Alexander Jannaeus was the first Maccabean ruler to proclaim himself as King on his coins, which he did in Hebrew, Greek, and occasionally in Aramaic. His capital was in Jerusalem.

Jerusalem During the Jewish Wars

116   117

116. Jewish War silver shekel year 2, struck 67/68 CE at Jerusalem.

Obverse: ⲖⲦⲰⲞⲢⲦ ⲖⲢⲰ (שקל ישראל, *shekel of Israel*); ⲦⲰ (שב, *year 2*) above ritual chalice with pearled rim, the base is raised by projections on ends.

Reverse: ⲈⲰ⊦ⲢⲒⲈ ⲰⲦⲌⲰⲢⲒⲦ (ירושלם הקדשה, *Jerusalem the holy*); staff with three pomegranate buds, round base.

ANS Collection: 2010.69.5. Gift of Abraham and Marion Sofaer.

"Jerusalem the holy" was used as a slogan on the coins of the Jewish War against Rome (66-70 CE). This slogan appeared on all of the silver shekels and half shekels struck during the five years of the war.

117. Jewish War bronze prutah year 2 struck at Jerusalem.

Obverse: ⲨⲦⲭⲰ ⲭⲦⲰ (שנת שתים, *year two)*; amphora with broad rim and two handles.

Reverse: Ⲏ⊦ⲞⲢ ⲭ⁹Ⲃ (חרת ציון, *the freedom of Zion)*; vine leaf on small branch with tendril.

ANS Collection: 2010.69.11. Gift of Abraham and Marion Sofaer.

On this coin the name "Zion" refers to Jerusalem.

118

118. Bar Kokhba Revolt (132 – 135 CE) bronze, struck 133/134 CE.
   Obverse: ᗷLW⋟9ᒣ (ירושלם, *Jerusalem*) within a wreath.
   Reverse: Lᖯ9ᙡᒣ 9ᗷL ᒐᙡ (שב לחר ישראל, *year two of the freedom of Israel*); amphora with two handles.
   ANS Collection: 2010.76.61. Gift of Abraham and Marion Sofaer.

   Although Bar Kokhba apparently never captured Jerusalem, the goal of his campaign was to regain control of the Holy City and to rebuild the Temple. The images of the Temple on his coins are seen as striving for his ultimate goal, which he did not achieve.

119

119. Bar Kokhba Revolt (132 – 135 CE) silver sela, struck 133/134 CE.
   Obverse: ᗷLW⋟9ᒣ (ירושלם, *Jerusalem*) on three sides of facade of Jerusalem Temple, ark or showbread table (?) seen from end in center of entrance.
   Reverse: Lᖯ9ᙡᒣ 9ᗷL ᒐᙡ (שב לחר ישראל, *year two of the freedom of Israel*); *lulav* with *etrog* at l.
   ANS Collection: 2010.76.33. Gift of Abraham and Marion Sofaer.

120

120. Bar Kokhba Revolt silver sela, struck 134/135 CE.

Obverse: שמעון (שמעון, *Simon*) on two sides; star above facade of the Jerusalem Temple, ark or showbread table (?) seen from end in center of entrance.

Reverse: לחרות ירושלם (לחרות ירושלם, *for the freedom of Jerusalem*); *lulav* with *etrog* at l.

ANS Collection: 2010.76.107. Gift of Abraham and Marion Sofaer.

121

121. Bar Kokhba Revolt silver sela, struck 134/135 CE.

Obverse: שמעון (שמעון, *Simon*) on two sides; wavy line above facade of the Jerusalem Temple, ark or showbread table (?) seen from end in center of entrance.

Reverse: לחרות ירושלם (לחרות ירושלם, *for the freedom of Jerusalem*); *lulav* with *etrog* at l.

ANS Collection: 2010.76.110. Gift of Abraham and Marion Sofaer.

Fig. 25.   Reconstructed view of the Jerusalem Temple looking toward the entrance to the sanctuary. This image shows both the golden vine, which appears on some Bar Kokhba coins as a wavy line, and the twinkling golden chandelier donated by Helena, queen of Adiabene, depicted as a cross or star because of the rays of light it emitted. The twelve steps to the Temple are also represented on the coin as a kind of horizontal ladder below the Temple. Courtesy Guide to Biblical Coins 5th Edition, Image by I. Goldstein and J.P. Fontanille.

Jerusalem as Aelia Capitolina

On the site of the Jerusalem Temple, Hadrian built a temple dedicated to Jupiter Capitolinus. Hadrian also re-founded Jerusalem as a Roman colony. It was Roman tradition to "re-found" a captured city; in the process, the Emperor ceremonially plowed a furrow around the city using a plow drawn by a cow and a bull. Hadrian re-named Jerusalem Colonia Aelia Capitolina after his ancestor Aelius, and one of his patron gods Jupiter Capitolinus. The name Aelia Capitolina appears on all of the coins struck in Jerusalem from 130 to 251 CE.

122   123

122. Hadrian (117-138 CE) bronze coin of Aelia Capitolina.

> Obverse: Draped bust of Hadrian r., laureate; IMP CAES TRAI HADRIANO AVG PP (Hadrian's royal name).
>
> Reverse: The emperor as founder, plowing r. with ox and cow; in background, vexillum; COL AEL KA PIT (*Colony of Aelia Capitolina*); in exergue, COND (*foundation*).
>
> *Courtesy The Abraham D. Sofaer Collection on loan at the ANS.*
>
> *Hadrian was the first of sixteen different emperors whose names appear on coins of Jerusalem during the Roman period.*

123. Hadrian bronze coin of Aelia Capitolina.

> Obverse: Draped bust of Hadrian r., laureate; IMP CAES TRAI HADRIANO AVG PP (Hadrian's royal name).
>
> Reverse: Facade of distyle temple; within, in center, Jupiter seated l., resting on scepter, flanked by Minerva on l. and Juno on r.; COL AEL KAP (*Colony of Aelia Capitolina*).
>
> *Courtesy The Abraham D. Sofaer Collection on loan at the ANS.*

Byzantine Jerusalem

124

124. Heraclius (610 – 641 CE) Jerusalem bronze follis.
    Obverse: Crowned bust of Heraclius facing;
    DN HERACLIVS PP AVG (Heraclius' royal name).
    Reverse: M; above, cross; on l. and r., date: ANNO II II (*year 4*) =
    613/614 CE; below, IEPOCOΛ (*Jerusalem*).
    Courtesy The Abraham D. Sofaer Collection on loan at the ANS.
    *This is the only year that Byzantine coins were struck in Jerusalem. An-
    other version of the same coin type of Heraclius carries the Greek for
    "Victory of God (Jesus)" in place of Jerusalem. Possibly these coins
    were minted to encourage the Christian defenders of the city during a
    siege by pagans.*

Umayyad Jerusalem as Ilya

125   126

125. Umayyad Jerusalem, Arab-Byzantine bronze follis, 7th century
    CE.
    Obverse: Standing facing imperial figure; on l., CONO...
    Reverse: M; Greek inscription: on l., IEPO; on r., COΛV; be-
    low, MWN (*of the people of Jerusalem*).
    Courtesy The Abraham D. Sofaer Collection on loan at the ANS.

126. Umayyad Jerusalem, Arab-Byzantine bronze fals, 7th century
CE.

> Obverse: Bearded figure of the caliph standing facing, wearing
> long robe, placing hand on his sword; Arabic inscription:
> لا اله الا االله وحده (*there is no god but God alone*).
> Reverse: M; below, exergual line; Arabic inscription, on l., ايليا
> (*Iliya*), on r., فلسطين (*Filastin*).
> *Courtesy The Abraham D. Sofaer Collection on loan at the ANS.*

Umayyad Coins with Menorah

During the Umayyad Period, this Islamic coin depicting the menorah
was struck in or near Jerusalem. This five- or seven-branched candle-
stick was an adoption by the Islamic mint authorities of the Jewish
menorah motif. It is not known why this design was used; perhaps the
designers or die-makers were Jewish artisans. It is also possible that
this particular series of coins was connected to a specific event, such
as the completion of the al-Aqsa Mosque around 715/716 CE. This
coin is an interesting testimony to the struggle for Jerusalem through
the ages.

127. Umayyad bronze coin, c. 7th – 8th centuries CE.

> Obverse: Seven-branched candlestick with flat base; around,
> Arabic inscription: لا اله الا االله وحده (*there is no god but God alone*).
> Reverse: Inscription in three lines: محمد / رسول / االله (*Muhammad
> is the Messenger of God*).
> *Courtesy The Abraham D. Sofaer Collection on loan at the ANS.*

128. Umayyad bronze coin, c. 7th – 8th centuries CE.

> Obverse: Five-branched candlestick with high base; around,
> Arabic inscription: لا اله الا االله وحده (*there is no god but God alone*).
> Reverse: Inscription in three lines: محمد / رسول / االله (*Muhammad
> is the Messenger of God*).
> *Courtesy The Abraham D. Sofaer Collection on loan at the ANS.*

Abbasid Jerusalem as al Quds

The Arabic name for Jerusalem is *al Quds*, "The Noble, Sacred Place."

129

129. Abbasid al Quds (*Jerusalem*), bronze fals, struck 832 CE.
Obverse: Inscription in three lines with two crescents below, surrounded by a cable border:
لا اله الا / ه وحد / ه لا شريك له (there is no god, but God alone, He has no associate).
Reverse: Inscription in three lines, in circle: محمد / رسول / الله (*Muhammad is the Messenger of God*); marginal inscription:
بسم الله ضرب هذا الفلس بالقدس سنة سبع عشر و مائتين (*in the name of God, this fals was struck at al- Quds in the year 217 = 832 CE*).
Courtesy The Abraham D. Sofaer Collection on loan at the ANS.

Crusader Jerusalem

The first Crusaders arrived in the Holy Land in June of 1099 and Jerusalem was captured on July 15. Pope Urban II promoted the First Crusade at the Council of Clermont in 1095; its goal was assisting the Byzantine Empire against the invading Seljuk Turks. Soon the goal was changed to the liberation of the Holy Land for Christians. The Crusader Kingdom of Jerusalem lasted nearly 200 years, until 1291, when the last Crusader fortress, Acre (today's Akko) was destroyed by the Mamluks.

The Crusader Kingdom of Jerusalem was a loose collection of towns, cities, and fortresses captured and established during the Crusades. At the strongest point it encompassed much of modern day Israel, Lebanon, and the Palestinian territories, as well as some authority in other crusader states such as Tripoli, Antioch, and Edessa.

Baldwin III (1130 – 1163) was king of Jerusalem from 1143 to 1163. He was among the second generation of the descendents of the original crusaders. Baldwin was only 13 years old when his father King Fulk of Anjou died, and the kingdom legally passed to his mother Melisende as the daughter of Baldwin II. She had ruled with Fulk as a consort, and Baldwin was crowned co-ruler and heir to his mother.

130   131   132

130. Baldwin III silver denier.
    Obverse: Cross in a ring; ✠ REX BALDVINVS (King Baldwin).
    Reverse: Tower of David in a ring; ✠ ƋE IERVSALEM (of Jerusalem).
    Courtesy The Abraham D. Sofaer Collection on loan at the ANS.

Amaury I of Jerusalem (1163 – July 11, 1174) was count of Jaffa and Ascalon , and from 1162 to 1174 King of Jerusalem. He was the second son of King Fulk and Melisende and younger brother of King Baldwin III. Amaury ascended to the throne of Jerusalem after his brother's death.

131. Amaury I silver denier.
    Obverse: Cross in a ring; ✠ REX AMALRICVS (King Amaury).
    Reverse: Church of the Holy Sepulchre in a ring: ✠ DE IERVSA-
    LEM.
    Courtesy The Abraham D. Sofaer Collection on loan at the ANS.

132. Anonymous Crusader Jerusalem silver denier, 12th century CE.
    Obverse: Cross in a ring; ✠ CRVCIS (retrograde civitas crucis, *city of the cross*).
    Reverse: Patriarchal cross on pedestal above a building (?), between two branches and two stars (monument of Golgotha?).
    Courtesy The Abraham D. Sofaer Collection on loan at the ANS.
    It is possible that this coin is intended to portray a monument constructed at the time on Golgotha, near the Church of the Holy Sepulchre.

Fig. 26. Tower of David, Jerusalem. Photograph by David Hendin

Fig 27. Illuminated manuscript of the coronation of Amaury I, c. 15th century. Courtesy Bibliothèque Nationale, France.

133

133. Anonymous Crusader Jerusalem, 12ᵗʰ century CE, silver denier.
　　Obverse:　Cross in a ring; SANA CRCA (?) (*Sancta Aerea = sacred area*).
　　Reverse:　Central building of the church of the Holy Sepulchre, between two towers or aedicule of the tomb of Jesus flanked by corner posts.
　　Courtesy The Abraham D. Sofaer Collection on loan at the ANS.
　　Another interpretation of the design on this rare coin is that it is a small shrine upon the tomb of Jesus, flanked by corner posts.

Fig. 28.　Church of the Holy Sepulchre interior in the 19ᵗʰ century. ANS Collection, photograph by Felix Bonfils.

134   135

134. Anonymous Crusader Jerusalem, 12th century CE, base silver de-
     nier.
     Obverse: Tower of David with balconies; ✠ TVRRIS DAVID (retro-
     grade) (*Tower of David*).
     Reverse: Sarcophagus and aedicule of the tomb of Jesus in the
     Holy Sepulchre church; unclear inscription [SEPVLChRVM DO-
     MINI?] (*Sepulchre of Our Lord*).
     Courtesy The Abraham D. Sofaer Collection on loan at the ANS.
     This is possibly part of an emergency coinage struck during the siege of
     Jerusalem by Saladin in 1187.

Raymond was a first cousin of Amaury I, and originally was Count
of Tripoli. However, after Amaury's death he became Regent of Jerusalem (1174 – 1177).

135. Baronial Coinage of Raymond of Tripoli, struck 1184 – 1186,
     bronze pougeoise.
     Obverse: Tower of David flanked by two dots, in a ring;
     T · V · R · R · I · S · (tower).
     Reverse: Eight pointed star in a ring; ✠ · D · A · V · I · T · (David).
     Courtesy The Abraham D. Sofaer Collection on loan at the ANS.

John of Brienne (c. 1170 – 1237) was originally Jean de Candia-Nev-
ers, count of Brienne, a French nobleman who became John I King of
Jerusalem by marriage, and John I Latin Emperor of Constantinople.

136

136. John of Brienne silver gros, struck 1210 – 1217 CE.
     Obverse: Cross in a ring; ✠IOHANNES REX (*King John*).
     Reverse: Church of the Holy Sepulchre in a ring; ✠ DE IERVSA-
     LEM.
     Courtesy The Abraham D. Sofaer Collection on loan at the ANS.

137

137. Crusader Jerusalem lead seal impression, 12th-13th centuries CE.
    Obverse: Inscription in five lines: 7 / SCE ‡ FRA / TNITATIS / DE IHERU / M (sigillum sanctae fraternitatis de iherusalem = *seal of the sacred fraternity of Jerusalem*).
    Reverse: Patriarchal cross in oval frame.
    Courtesy The Abraham D. Sofaer Collection on loan at the ANS.
    The seal from which this was made probably belonged to a Jerusalemite Crusader fraternity such as the St. Mary Hospital of Josaphat or St. John. This impression formerly belonged to the Biblical Museum of Saint Anne in Jerusalem.

138

138. Crusader Acre (Akko) lead seal impression, 12th-13th centuries CE.
    Obverse: Two figures with halos; on l., S /P (*St. Peter*); on r., S /A (*St. Andrew*); marginal inscription: @ ELEMOSINA · FRATER-NITATIS · ACCO · (*Almonry of the Fraternity of Acco*).
    Reverse: The Church of the Holy Sepulchre with Templum Domini inside; in upper l. field, sun and on r., moon; mar- ginal inscription: @ IN · HONORE · DI · 1 · XPIAVITA TIS · (*in honor of the god of the Christians*).
    Courtesy The Abraham D. Sofaer Collection on loan at the ANS.

GODS, GODDESSES, AND MONUMENTS ON THE CITY COINS

Even before the first Maccabean coins, important cities in ancient Israel struck coins. Many more were issued after Augustus, by cities under Roman rule. These powers were granted to promote both loyalty to Rome and commerce in the area. The city coins also developed as a means of local economic, political, and cultural expression.

Thirty-eight cities of ancient Israel, Transjordan, and the Province of Arabia issued coins. This is not a large number compared to more than 350 cities in Asia Minor and around 90 more in Greece and its islands. City coinage came to an end during the reign of Gallienus, about 268 CE when empire-wide reform of Roman coinage rendered civic coinage redundant.

Although these coins were issued during the Roman period, we may keep in mind that most of the cities were quite ancient, and many are mentioned in the Old Testament, New Testament, Talmud, or Josephus.

GALILEE AND SAMARIA

Akko (Ake, Acre, Ptolemais)

Asher drove not out the inhabitants of Akko – JUDGES 1:31.

139

139. Salonina, wife of Gallienus (253 – 268 CE), bronze.

> *Obverse:* Draped bust of Salonina r. seen from rear.; CORNEL SALONINA AVG (Salonina's royal name).
>
> *Reverse:* Zeus Heliopolites (the Ba'al of Carmel) in portable shrine, surrounded by Zodiac wheel; around shrine: COL PTOL (*colony of Ptolemais*).
>
> *Courtesy The Abraham D. Sofaer Collection on loan at the ANS.*

Fig. 29. Mosaic floor showing Zodaic on synagogue floor at Beit Alpha, 5th-6th centuries CE. Photograph Meshorer, TestiMoney.

Caesarea Marítima

Which when the brethren knew, they brought him down to Caesarea and sent him forth to Tarsus – ACTS 9:30.

140

140. Trajan (98 – 117 CE) bronze coin.
>   Obverse: Bust of Trajan r., laureate; IMP CAES NER TRAIA-NO. OP AVG GER DAC COS VI P.P (Trajan's royal name).
>   Reverse: Tetrastyle temple with central arch standing behind enclosure with altar in front; within, Tyche standing l., holding bust and scepter, resting foot on helmet; at her feet in r. field, harbor-god holding anchor; C I F AVG /CAES (*Imperial royal Flavian colony of Caesarea*).
>   *Courtesy The Abraham D. Sofaer Collection on loan at the ANS.*

Panias, (Caesarea Philippi, Baniyas)

When Jesus came into the coasts of Caesarea Philippi, he asked his disciples, saying, 'whom do men say that I, the Son of Man, am?' – MATTHEW 16:13.

141

141. Julia Maesa, grandmother of Elagabalus (218 – 222 CE), struck 220 CE

   Obverse: Draped bust of Julia Maesa r.; ΙΟΥΛΙΑ ΜΕϹ ΑΥΓ (Julia's royal name).

   Reverse: Pan standing nude facing, looking r., playing the flute;on his r., tree trunk with syrinx hung on its lower part and pedum at foot of tree; in semi circular colonnaded area with fence in front; in exergue, ΚΑΙ Π ϹΕ ΙΕ ΑϹΥ ϹΚΓ (*of Caesarea Panias holy and inviolate, year 223* = 220 CE).

   Courtesy The Abraham D. Sofaer Collection on loan at the ANS.

Fig. 30. Panias springs today with ancient niches for statues and cave of Pan in background. Photograph by Gugganij.

Joppa (Jaffa, Yafo)

I was in the city of Joppa praying: and in a trance I saw a vision, A certain vessel descend, as it had been a great sheet, let down from heaven by four corners – ACTS 11:5.

142

142. Caracalla (198 – 217 CE) bronze.
    Obverse: Bust of Caracalla r., laureate; inscription: AYT KAI ANTWNINOC (Caracalla's royal name).
    Reverse: Perseus standing r., wearing Phrygian hat and winged sandals, holding harpa and the head of Medusa in extended r.; retrograde inscription (starting on r.), ΦΛ ΙΟΠΠΗC (*Flavia Joppa*).
    Courtesy The Abraham D. Sofaer Collection on loan at the ANS.

Neapolis (Nablus, Shechem)

And Abram passed through the land unto the place of Shechem, unto the terebinth of Moreh – Genesis 12:6.

143

143. Antoninus Pius (138 – 161 CE) bronze medallion, struck 158/159 CE.

Obverse: Draped bust of Antoninus Pius r., laureate; AYTOK KAICAP ANTWNINOC CEBAC EYCE (Antoninus Pius' royal name).

Reverse: View of Mount Gerizim; below in front, a colonnade with two arched entrances; the l. one leads to a stairway on l., flanked by a series of shrines or altars on the slope; the stairway leads to a temple seen in three quarter view; another roadway flanked by trees leads from the colonnade to an altar on top of the hill to the r.; ΦΛ ΝΕΑС ΠΟΛΕΟС СΥΡΙΑС ΠΑΛΑΙСΤΙΝΗС (*Flavian Palestine in Syria Palestina*); in exergue, date: ET ΠΖ (*year 87* = 158/159 CE).

Courtesy Israel Museum, Jerusalem: Gift of Abraham and Marion Sofaer.

144

144. Otacilia Severa, wife of Philip I (244 – 249 CE) bronze.

Obverse: Draped bust of Otacilia Severa r., on crescent; M OT SEVERAE AVG M C (Otacilia's royal name).

Reverse: Male figure, named as the Decanos, walking r., carrying small altar or modius and holding lily scepter; in r. field, star; above, Mount Gerizim; on l., ΔΕΚΑΝΟΣ (Decanos); in exergue, COL; on l., NEAPOL; on r., NEOCORO.

Courtesy Israel Museum, Jerusalem: Gift of Abraham and Marion Sofaer.

The Decanos was one of 36 Decans responsible for the 360 degrees of the Zodiac, in other words, responsible for the fate of the world. This is the only depiction of a Decanos on coins, and it suggests that there might have been a special cult of the 36 decans at Neapolis.

145

145. Philip I and Philip II (247 – 249 CE) bronze.

Obverse: Jugate busts of Philip I and Philip II r., both draped and laureate; IIMM CC P FILIPPIS AVGG (their royal names).

Reverse: At l., figure standing r. with hand raised to lips; facing her a figure standing l., holding a kneeling figure and a sword or knife; to r. a forth figure advancing l. and raising hand, and at side, ram l.; in exergue, COL; on l., NEAPOL; on r., NEO-CORO.

Courtesy Israel Museum, Jerusalem: Gift of Abraham and Marion Sofaer.

This scene is interpreted as the binding of Isaac by his father Abraham who, in the end, sacrificed a ram instead.

Fig. 31.   The binding of Isaac on a mosaic floor from the synagogue at Beit Alpha, 5th–6th centuries CE Photograph: Meshorer, TestiMoney.

Sepphoris (Diocaesarea, Zippori)

R. Jose says: Also any whose name was signed as a witness in the old archives at Sepphoris – MISHNAH, KIDDUSHIN 4:5.

146. Trajan (98 – 117 CE) bronze.
   Obverse: Head of Trajan r., laureate; ΤΡΑΙΑΝΟΣ ΑΥΤΟΚΡΑΤΩΡ ΕΔΩΚΕΝ (*the Emperor Trajan gave*).
   Reverse: Palm tree; below, ΣΕΠΦΩ / ΡΗΝΩΝ (*Sepphoris*).
   Courtesy The Abraham D. Sofaer Collection on loan at the ANS.

Tiberias (Tveriah)

Howbeit there came other boats from Tiberias nigh unto the place where they did eat bread, after that the Lord had given thanks – JOHN 6:23.

147. Trajan (98 – 117 CE) bronze coin struck 108/109 CE.
   Obverse: Head of Trajan r., laureate; ΑΥΤΟΚΡ ΚΑΙC ΝΕΡ · ΤΡΑΙΑΝΟC CΕΒ ΓΕΡΜ (Trajan's royal name).
   Reverse: Hygieia seated r. on rock below which water is flowing, feeding snake from bowl; ΤΙΒΕΡΙ ΚΛΑΥΔΙ (*Claudian Tiberias*); across field, date: ΕΤ Ч (*year 90* = 108/109 CE).
   Courtesy The Abraham D. Sofaer Collection on loan at the ANS.
   Tiberias was built upon a number of hot springs which in ancient times— and today—were believed to have special medicinal value. Hence the images of Hygieia, goddess of health, and Poseidon, god of the sea, were promotional references to the city.

JUDAEA, IDUMAEA, AND PHILISTIA

Aelia Capitolina (Jerusalem)

Pray for the peace of Jerusalem; May they prosper that love thee. Peace be within thy walls, And prosperity within thy palaces – PSALMS 122: 6-7.

Three coins of Antoninus Pius (138 – 161 CE) depicting symbols of the Tenth Roman Legion, the boar, legionary eagle, and war galley with abbreviations for the name of the city. After the Jewish War (66 – 70 CE) the Tenth Roman Legion was garrisoned here, and remained a force in the city for hundreds of years.

148.

> Obverse: Draped bust of Antoninus Pius r., laureate; IMP CAES H ANTONINO (Pius' royal name).
>
> Reverse: Boar standing r.; K A C (*Colony Aelia Capitolina*).
> *Courtesy The Abraham D. Sofaer Collection on loan at the ANS.*

149.

> Obverse: Draped bust of Antoninus Pius r., laureate; IMP CAES H ANTONINO (Pius' royal name).
>
> Reverse: Legionary eagle r.; above, COL AELCAP (*Colony Aelia Capitolina*).
> *Courtesy The Abraham D. Sofaer Collection on loan at the ANS.*

150.

> Obverse: Draped bust of Antoninus Pius r., laureate; IM ANTO-NIN (Pius' royal name).
>
> Reverse: War-galley sailing r.; above, K A C (*Colony Aelia Capitolina*).
> *Courtesy The Abraham D. Sofaer Collection on loan at the ANS.*

Ascalon (Ashkelon)

Tell it not in Gath, Publish it not in the streets of Ashkelon;
Lest the daughters of the Philistines rejoice – 2 SAMUEL 1:20.

151

151. Septimius Severus (193 – 211 CE) bronze.
   Obverse: Draped bust of Septimius Severus r., laureate; AV KA
   C CEOVHP[...]CEB (Severus' royal name).
   Reverse: Building with four doorways, one within the other,
   and Egyptian style columns (temple of Phanebal?); on l. and
   r., ACK AΛW (*Ascalon*); in exergue, date: ΘT (309 = 205/206
   CE).

   Courtesy Israel Museum, Jerusalem: Gift of Abraham and Marion Sofaer.

Ascalon was a Canaanite city-state under Egyptian influence, and
the Egyptian style is shown on many of its coins. The local goddess
Derketo was part woman and part fish.

Gaza (Aza)

And Samson went to Gaza, and saw there a harlot, and
went in unto her – JUDGES 16:1.

152

152. Hadrian (117 – 138 CE) bronze coin struck 135/136 CE.

Obverse: Bust of Hadrian l., laureate; ΑΥΤ ΚΑΙ ΤΡΑΙ ΑΔΡΙΑΝΟC CE (Hadrian's royal name).

Reverse: Distyle facade of the temple of Marnas; in- side, Marnas on r. standing l., holding bow and branch, looking at Artemis standing r., holding bow and drawing arrow from quiver at her shoulder; on l., ΓΑΖΑ (Gaza); on r., ΜΑΡΝΑ (Marnas); in exergue, date: Ζ ΕΠΙ ϚϤΡ ᛡ ([year] 7 of the visit, 196 = 135/136 CE.

Courtesy The Abraham D. Sofaer Collection on loan at the ANS.

The coins of Gaza are dated according to the time of Hadrian's visit to Judaea in 129/130 CE. The Phoenician letter ᛡ (mem), used as a mintmark by Gaza, is the first letter of the name of the city's special god Marnas, who was a local version of Zeus.

THE DECAPOLIS AND PROVINCIA ARABIA

Abila (Abel)

It happened with a water-channel in Abel that they used to draw from it on the Sabbath by the consent of the elders – MISHNAH, ERUBIN 8: 7.

153

153. Marcus Aurelius (161 – 180 CE) bronze, struck 161/162 CE.

Obverse: Draped and cuirassed bust of Marcus Aurelius r., laureate; ΑΥΤ ΚΑΙC Μ ΑΥΡ ΑΝΤ ΑΥΓ (M. Aurelius' royal name).

Reverse: Heracles, nude, seated on rock l., resting hand on club and leaning on the rock; CE ΑΒΙΛΗΝΩΝ Ι. Α.Α.Γ ΚΟΙ CY (*of the people of Seleucia Abila, holy, city of asylum, autonomous, which is in Coele-Syria*); in exergue, date: ΕΚC (*225 = 161/2 CE*).

Courtesy The Abraham D. Sofaer Collection on loan at the ANS.

Capitolias (Beit Reisha)

154

154. Marcus Aurelius (161 – 180 CE) bronze struck 166/167 CE.

Obverse: Draped and cuirassed bust of Marcus Aurelius r., laureate, seen from rear; AYT KAIC M AYP ANTWNEINOC (M. Aurelius' royal name.)

Reverse: Hexastyle temple with central arch; within, Tyche standing l. in short dress, resting foot on helmet (?), holding bust and long scepter; at her feet, river god swimming; inscription starting in exergue, KAΠITOΛIEWN I A A (*of the people of Capitolias, holy, city of asylum, autonomous*). O ([year] 70) = 166/167 CE or 167/168 CE).

Courtesy The Abraham D. Sofaer Collection on loan at the ANS.

Gadara (Gader, Hammat Gader)

Then the whole multitude of the country of the Gadarenes round about besought him to depart from them – LUKE 8:37.

155

155. Marcus Aurelius (161 – 180 CE) bronze medallion struck
     160/161 CE.

     Obverse: Bust of Marcus Aurelius r., laureate; AYT KAIC M AYP
     ANTWNEINOC (M. Aurelius' royal name).

     Reverse: Galley sailing l., navigator at stern and standard-bearer
     in front; above, ΓΑΔΑΡΕWN / NAYMA (*Gadara, Naumachia*); in
     exergue, date: ΔΚC (224 = 160/161 CE).

     Courtesy Israel Museum, Jerusalem: Gift of Abraham and Marion Sofaer.

     *Gadara was located on the heights above the Yarmuk River, near the Sea
     of Galilee. The city's maritime character is shown by its coins which
     depicted warships for more than 200 years. This medallion commemo-
     rates the Naumachia, a festive event in which a mock naval battle sym-
     bolizing Pompey's conquest of the country was staged.*

Gerasa (Gerash)

But Alexander [Jannaeus], when he had taken Pella,
marched to Gerasa again out of the covetous desire he had
of Theodorus's possessions – JOSEPHUS, JEWISH WARS, 1, 4:8.

156

156. Marcus Aurelius (161 – 180 CE) bronze.

     Obverse: Draped and cuirassed bust of Marcus Aurelius r., seen
     from rear, laureate; AYTO KAIC M AVP ANTW (M. Aurelius'
     royal name).

     Reverse: Artemis Huntress advancing r., drawing arrow from
     quiver and holding bow, hound running r. at her feet; AP-
     TEMIC TYXH ΓEP (*Artemis-Tyche of Gerasa*).

     Courtesy The Abraham D. Sofaer Collection on loan at the ANS.

Hippos (Susita, Tob)

Then Jephthah fled from his brethren, and dwelt in the land
of Tob – JUDGES 11:3.

157

157. Commodus (197 – 192 CE) bronze, struck 184/185 CE.
Obverse: Bust of Commodus r., laureate; AYT K M AYP KOM
ANTW (Commodus' royal name).
Reverse: Tyche standing l., holding horse by bridle and cornu-
copia; ANTIOX ΠΡ ΙΠ ΙΕΡ ΑϹΥΛ (*of the Antiocheans at Hippos,
holy, city of asylum*); in exergue, date: HMC (*248 = 184/185*).
Courtesy The Abraham D. Sofaer Collection on loan at the ANS.

Nysa-Scythopolis (Beit Shean, Beisan)

And they put his armor in the house of the Ashtaroth; and
fastened his body to the wall of Beth-shean – I SAMUEL 31:10.

158

158. Gordian III (238 – 244 CE) bronze struck 240/241 CE.
Obverse: Draped and cuirassed bust of Gordian III r., seen from
rear, laureate; AVT K M ANT ΓΟΡΔΙΑΝΟϹ ϹΕΒ (Gordian's
royal name).
Reverse: Nysa-Tyche seated r. on throne with infant Dionysos in
her arms; NYC CKVΘOΠO IEPA (*of Nysa Scythopolis, holy, city
of asylum*); in exergue, date: ΔΤ (*304 = 240/241 CE*).
Courtesy The Abraham D. Sofaer Collection on loan at the ANS.
*According to local legends, Nysa, the nurse of the god Dionysus, was born
here, and the city takes part of its name after her.*

Pella (Pehal)

> But Alexander [Jannaeus], when he had taken Pella…
> – JOSEPHUS, WARS I, 4:8.

159

159. Commodus (177 – 192 CE) bronze struck 183/184 CE.

Obverse: Draped and cuirassed bust of Commodus r., seen from rear, laureate; AV K M KOMMOΔOC ANTWNINOC (Commodus' royal name).

Reverse: Acropolis of Pella with hexastyle temple and figure standing in center; the temple is placed on podium supported by pillars; at the base of mountain, a colonnade with gateways; ΦΙΛΙΠ Τ Κ ΠΕΛΛΑΙΟΝ Π ΝΥΦ Κ CΥ ΕΛ (*of the people of Philippopolis which is also Pella at the Nymphaeum in Coele-Syria, free [city]*); in exergue, date: ETO ϚMC (*year 246* = 183/184 CE.)

Courtesy The Abraham D. Sofaer Collection on loan at the ANS.

PRICES AND VALUES

The *shekel* denomination is equivalent to the *tetradrachm* or *sela*. It is made up of four *quarters*. Each *quarter* is also called a *zuz*, *drachm*, or *denarius* (plural, *denarii*).

Each *shekel* contained around 256 bronze *prutah* coins (plural, *prutot*), a number that varied in different periods.

We can better understand the value of these coins by exploring the New Testament, Josephus, and Rabbinical sources such as the Talmud. For example:

•Wages. In the early first century, Rabbi Hillel's daily wage was one-half *denarius*. A good scribe earned 12 *denarii* per week. Scribes were paid a few *prutot* to write each normal document.

•Bread. In the first and second centuries CE, a loaf of bread cost around 16 *prutot*, while a small loaf cost only 8 *prutot*.

•Olive oil. Josephus reported that one amphora of olive oil from the Galilee cost one *drachm* or one *denarius*.

•Fruit. In the first to second centuries CE the price of one pomegranate was between one and eight *prutot*. A cluster of grapes or figs cost eight *prutot*, and a cucumber, a rare delicacy, cost a *denarius*.

•Livestock. In the first to second centuries CE, an ox cost 100 *denarii*, but a calf cost only 20 *denarii*. A newborn donkey cost two to four *denarii*, as did a lamb. In Jerusalem, two sparrows cost around 14 *prutot*.

•The cheapest meal for a bridegroom, who would surely dine lavishly, cost one *denarius*, but a modest meal of a small roll, a plate of lentils, two pieces of meat, and two glasses of wine cost around 20 *prutot*.

•Several oil lamps and wicks cost only one *prutah*.

In ancient times, as today, inflation and laws of supply and demand moved prices for comparable commodities at different times.

Mints of the
Holy Land

MACCABEE FAMILY TREE (PARTIAL)

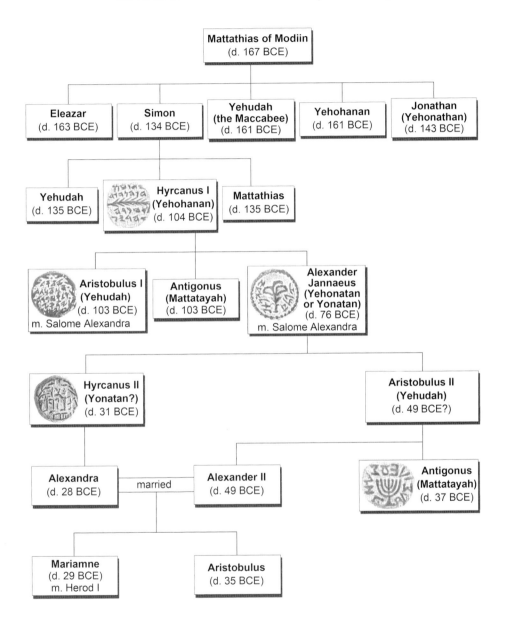

HERODIAN FAMILY TREE (Partial)

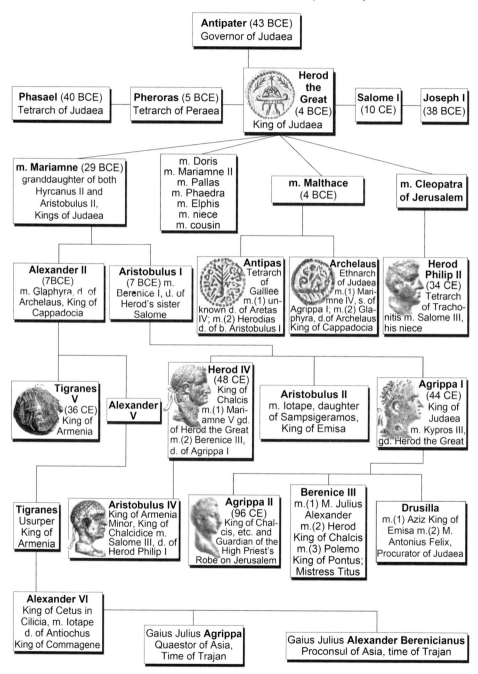

Antipater (43 BCE)
Governor of Judaea

Herod the Great (4 BCE)
King of Judaea

Phasael (40 BCE)
Tetrarch of Judaea

Pheroras (5 BCE)
Tetrarch of Peraea

Salome I (10 CE)

Joseph I (38 BCE)

m. Mariamne (29 BCE)
granddaughter of both Hyrcanus II and Aristobulus II, Kings of Judaea

m. Doris
m. Mariamne II
m. Pallas
m. Phaedra
m. Elphis
m. niece
m. cousin

m. Malthace (4 BCE)

m. Cleopatra of Jerusalem

Alexander II (7BCE)
m. Glaphyra, d. of Archelaus, King of Cappadocia

Aristobulus I (7 BCE) m. Berenice I, d. of Herod's sister Salome

Antipas
Tetrarch of Galilee m.(1) unknown d. of Aretas IV; m.(2) Herodias d. of b. Aristobulus I

Archelaus
Ethnarch of Judaea m.(1) Mariamne IV, s. of Agrippa I; m.(2) Glaphyra, d.of Archelaus King of Cappadocia

Herod Philip II (34 CE)
Tetrarch of Trachonitis m. Salome III, his niece

Tigranes V (36 CE)
King of Armenia

Alexander V

Herod IV (48 CE)
King of Chalcis m.(1) Mariamne V gd. of Herod the Great m.(2) Berenice III, d. of Agrippa I

Aristobulus II
m. Iotape, daughter of Sampsigeramos, King of Emisa

Agrippa I (44 CE)
King of Judaea m. Kypros III, gd. Herod the Great

Tigranes
Usurper King of Armenia

Aristobulus IV
King of Armenia Minor, King of Chalcidice m. Salome III, d. of Herod Philip I

Agrippa II (96 CE)
King of Chalcis, etc. and Guardian of the High Priest's Robe on Jerusalem

Berenice III
m.(1) M. Julius Alexander m.(2) Herod King of Chalcis m.(3) Polemo King of Pontus; Mistress Titus

Drusilla
m.(1) Aziz King of Emisa m.(2) M. Antonius Felix, Procurator of Judaea

Alexander VI
King of Cetus in Cilicia, m. Iotape d. of Antiochus King of Commagene

Gaius Julius **Agrippa**
Quaestor of Asia, Time of Trajan

Gaius Julius **Alexander Berenicianus**
Proconsul of Asia, time of Trajan

KEY: CAPS=Rulers or governor; ( )=dates of death; m.=married; d.=daughter; s.=sister; b.=brother; gd.=granddaughter; ()=spouse number Copyright 2010 by David Hendin

BIBLICAL-JUDAEAN COIN SYNOPSIS

5 – 3 Centuries BCE   Philisto Arabian, Yehud and Samarian Coins.

132 – 130 BCE   Maccabean-Seleucid coin of Hyrcanus I naming Antiochus VII struck in Jerusalem, dated ΑΠΡ (181) or ΒΠΡ (182) of the Seleucid Era (beginning 312 BCE) carries the name of Antiochus VII. Greek legends.

135 – 104 BCE   John Hyrcanus I struck bronze coins at the Jerusalem mint after 130 BCE. None were dated. His Hebrew name was *Yehohanan,* his title was High Priest. Paleo-Hebrew legends.

104 BCE   Judah Aristobulus I struck bronze coins at the Jerusalem mint. They are quite rare. None were dated. His Hebrew name was *Yehudah,* on the coins his title was High Priest, although Josephus notes he was the first Jewish ruler to hold the title "King." Paleo-Hebrew legends.

104 – 76 BCE   Alexander Jannaeus struck bronze coins at the Jerusalem mint. One coin was dated LKE "Year 25" (of Jannaeus) and was thus struck in 78 BCE. His Hebrew name was *Yehonatan* also spelled as *Yonatan.* Paleo-Hebrew, Aramaic and Greek legends.

76 – 67 BCE   Jannaeus' widow, Salome Alexandra, may have continued to issue the small prutah types (also known as 'mites') with irregular Greek and Aramaic legends. Hyrcanus II is High Priest during this period and we cannot rule out the possibility that coins possibly attributed to Hyrcanus II are issued at this time rather than later, after Salome Alexandra's death.

67 and 63 – 40 BCE   Hyrcanus II or his brother Aristobulus II may have struck coins with the name *Yonatan*. The brothers were in a frequent state of war with each other. Paleo-Hebrew legends.

58 BCE   Roman Republican denarius struck to commemorate the defeat of Aretas III by Pompey's general Marcus Scaurus. Aretas III supported Hyrcanus II in his battles against Aristobulus II. Latin legends.

40 – 37 BCE   Mattathias Antigonus, the final Maccabean king, strikes several denominations of bronze coins including the famous "menorah" coin. Paleo-Hebrew, Greek legends.

40 BCE – 4 BCE   Herod was named King by Rome in 40 BCE, but Antigonus was king on the ground. Herod's first coins were dated LΓ (year 3), possibly 37 CE, his first year as king on the ground, but the third year of his kingship. Greek legends.

4 BCE – 6 CE   Herod's son Archelaus reigns over Judaea as Ethnarch. His coins were probably struck in Jerusalem and are bronze and undated. Greek legends.

4 BCE – 40 CE   Herod's son Antipas issued a series of dated bronze coins as Tetrarch of Galilee and Peraea, the largely Jewish portion of Trans-Jordan. His major mint was in Tiberias, however a newly discovered coin of Antipas shows that he also issued at least one coin early in his reign, probably from a mint at Sepphoris, his first capital. Greek legends.

Antipas' coins are dated as follows:

Δ	4	1 BCE
LKΔ	24	20 CE
LΛΓ	33	29 CE
LΛΔ	34	30 CE
LΛZ	37	33 CE
LMΓ	39	35 CE

4 BCE – 34 CE   Herod's son Philip issued a series of dated bronze coins as Tetrarch of the northeast section of his father's kingdom. He founded the city of Caesarea Philippi, also called Paneas, which was his capital and mint. Greek legends.

Philip's coins are dated as follows:

LE	5	1/2 CE
LIB	12	8/9 CE
LIϛ	16	12/13 CE
LIΘ	19	15/16 CE
LΛ	30	26/27 CE
LΛΓ	33	29/30 CE
LΛΔ	34	30/31 CE
LΛZ	37	33/34 CE

37 – 44 CE   Agrippa I, grandson of Herod I and Mariamne the Hasmonean, issues coins in Jerusalem for the Jewish population as well as basic civic coins, probably at Paneas. Greek legends.

Agrippa I's coins are dated as follows:

LB	2	37/38 CE
LE	5	40/41 CE
Lϛ	6	41/42 CE
LZ	7	42/43 CE
LH	8	43/44 CE

41 – 48 CE   Herod of Chalcis, brother of Agrippa I, ruled the
              kingdom of Chalcis in Coele Syria, which had few
              or no Jews. However, he was given authority over the
              Jerusalem Temple and the selection of High Priests.
              Greek legends.

57 – 92 CE   Aristobulus of Chalcis, son of Herod of Chalcis. He
              married the infamous Salome, who earlier had danced
              before Herod Antipas and demanded (at her mother's
              insistence) the head of John the Baptist. Presumbly to
              celebrate his love for her, Aristobulus struck coins
              with Salome's portrait on the reverse. Salome's first
              husband was her uncle, Herod Philip, son of Herod
              I. His coins were dated to the Years 3 (56/67 CE), 8
              (61/62 CE), 13 (66/67 CE), and 17 (70/71 CE). Greek
              legends.

55 – 95 CE   Agrippa II, Herod I's great grandson, issued the most
              extensive series of coins struck by a Jewish ruler in
              Ancient Israel. Most carried Flavian portraits and
              were probably struck at several mints including Tibe-
              rias, Sepphoris, Caesarea Paneas, and Caesarea Mari-
              tima. Greek legends. There was a series of coins
              probably struck under Agrippa II, but before he be-
              came King: at Caesarea Paneas with the portraits of
              Claudius and Brittanicus, and Nero; at Caesarea Ma-
              ritima with portraits of Claudius, Nero and Agrippina
              II; at Tiberias resembling the coins of Herod Antipas;
              at Sepphoris in an interesting "Jewish" style, and the
              first coins mentioning Vespasian prior to his becoming
              emperor.
                   Agrippa II issued coins dated to two eras
              which have long been topics of debate. Alla Kushnir-Stein
              suggests that the eras began in 49 and 60 CE. The second era,
              may have begun when Agrippa II consolidated his fullest
              powers, though this is not very clear.

Agrippa II's era beginning 47 CE, mint of Caesarea Paneas.

Kς	26	74/75 CE
KZ	27	75/76 CE
KΘ	29	77/78 CE
Λ	30	78/79 CE
ΔΛ	34	82/83 CE
EΛ	35	83/84 CE

Agrippa II's era beginning 60 CE, mint of Caesarea Maritima.

ΔI	14	73/74 CE
IE	15	74/75 CE
HI	18	77/78 CE
IΘ	19	78/79 CE
KΔ	24	83/84 CE
KE	25	84/85 CE
Kς	26	85/86 CE
KΘ	29	88/89 CE

6 – 66 CE   Prefects and Procurators of Rome

Coins were dated to regnal years of the Emperors:

Coponius (6 – 9 CE) under Augustus
(With the name Caesar.)

Λς	36	6 CE

Marcus Ambibulus (9 – 12 CE) under Augustus
(With the name Caesar)

ΛΘ	39	9 CE
LM	40	10 CE
LMA	41	11 CE

Valerius Gratus (15 – 26 CE) under Tiberius
(With the names Tiberius, Tiberius Caesar and Caesar as well as Julia [Julia Livia, mother of Tiberius].

B	2	15/16 CE
Γ	3	16/17 CE
Δ	4	17/18 CE
E	5	18/19 CE
IA	11	24/25 CE

Pontius Pilate (26 – 36 CE) under Tiberius
(With the names Tiberius Caesar and Julia.)

Iς	16	29/30 CE
IZ	17	30/31 CE
IH	18	31/32 CE

Antonius Felix (52 – 59 CE) under Claudius
(With the names Julia Agrippina [wife of Claudius],
Tiberius Claudius Caesar Germanicus [royal name of
Claudius himself], Nero Claudius Caesar [son of
Claudius] and Britannicus [younger son of Claudius].

IΔ	14	54 CE

Porcius Festus (59 – 62 CE) under Nero

LE	5	58/59 CE

66 – 70 CE   The Jewish War

Ⴕ	1	66/67 CE
⅃	2	67/68 CE
⅂	3	68/69 CE
⅂	4	69/70 CE
Ⴒ	5	70/71 CE

132 – 135 CE   The Bar Kochba War

✕ᗺႵ	1	132/133 CE
⅃w	2	133/134 CE
Undated	3	134/135 CE

ILLUSTRATIONS

FURTHER READING

Ariel, D.T.
> In Press *The Coins of Herod*. Ancient Judaism and Early
> Christianity monograph series. Leiden: E.J. Brill.

Burnett, A., Amandry M., and Ripolles, P.
> 1992   *Roman Provincial Coinage*, Vol. I, Parts I and II.
> London: British Museum Press.
> 1998   *Roman Provincial Coinage*, Supp. I. London: British
> Museum Press.

Dayan, M.
> 1978   *Living with the Bible*. New York: William Morrow.

Fontanille, J.P. and Gosline, F.
> 2001   *The Coins of Pontius Pilate*. Warren Center, Pa.:
> Shangra La.

Gitler, H. and Tal, O.
> 2006   *The Coinage of Philistia of the Fifth and Fourth Centuries
> BC: A Study of the Earliest Coins of Palestine*. Milan:
> Ennerre/New York: Amphora.

Grant, M.
> 1971   *Herod the Great*. New York: American Heritage Press.
> 1973   *The Jews in the Roman World*. New York: Scribner's.
> 1974   *The Army of the Caesars*. New York: Scribner's.
> 1977   *Jesus: An Historian's Review of the Gospels*. New York:
> Scribner's.

Hendin, D.
> 2005   *Not Kosher, Forgeries of Ancient Jewish and Biblical Coins*.
> New York: Amphora
> 2007   *Ancient Scale Weights and Pre-Coinage Currency of the
> Near East*. New York: Amphora.
> 2010   *Guide to Biblical Coins 5th Edition*. New York: Amphora.

Josephus
   1981   *The Jewish War, G.A. Williamson (trans.), E. Mary Small-wood (revisions and notes)* London-New York: Penguin. 1959, 1981.

Matsson, G.O.
   1999   *The Gods, Goddesses, and Heroes of the Ancient Coins of Bible Lands.* Stockholm: Mälartyrckeriet AB.

Meshorer, Y.
   2000   *TestiMoney.* Jerusalem: Israel Museum.
   2001   *A Treasury of Jewish Coins (English).* New York: Amphora.

Meyers, C, *et al.*
   2000   *Women in Scripture.* New York: Houghton Mifflin.

Perlman, Moshe.
   1973   *The Maccabees.* New York: Macmillan 1973.

Romanoff, P.
   1944   *Jewish Symbols on Ancient Jewish Coins.* 1971 reprint. New York: American Israel Numismatic Assn.

Roth, C.
   1954   *History of the Jews.* New York: Schocken. 1961 reprint.

Smallwood, M.
   1981   *The Jews Under Roman Rule From Pompey to Diocletian: A Study in Political Relations.* Leiden, E.J. Brill.

Sperber, D.
   1974   *Roman Palestine 200–400 Money & Prices.* Ramat Gan: Bar Ilan University Press.

Vagi, David.
   1999   *Coinage and History of the Roman Empire*, Vols. 1 and 2. Sydney: Coin World.

Yadin, Y.
   1971   *Bar-Kokhba*, New York: Random House.

AMERICAN NUMISMATIC SOCIETY BOOKS

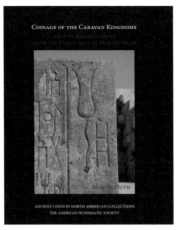

Coinage of the Caravan Kingdoms: Ancient Arabian Coins from the Collection of Martin Huth. (*Ancient Coins in North American Collections 10, 2010***).** ISBN-13: 978-0-89722-318-8. 188 pages, Hardcover. The Martin Huth collection of pre-Islamic coins, covering all parts of the Arabian Peninsula, represents the largest assembly of such material ever assembled, exceeding by far the holdings of existing museum collections. 480 coins are fully described and illustrated on more than 70 pages of plates. $150

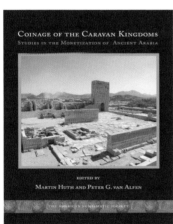

Coinage of the Caravan Kingdoms - Studies in the Monetization of Ancient Arabia by Martin Huth and Peter G. van Alfen (*Numismatic Studies No. 25, 2010*). ISBN-13: 978-0-89722-312-6. 602 pages, 42 plates, Hardcover. The first comprehensive look at ancient Arabian coinage since Hill's 1922 British Museum catalogue. Features updated typologies, die studies of the owl and Alexander imitations, and essays by numismatists, archaeologists, and epigraphists that situate the coins in their political, social, and economic contexts. $250

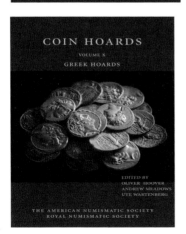

Coin Hoards X edited by Oliver Hoover, Andrew Meadows, Ute Wartenberg Kagan. ISBN 978-0-89722-315-7. 281 pages, 67 plates. The tenth volume of Coin Hoards is again focused on ancient Greek coinage. The inventory contains records of 471 new hoards or re-evaluations of old ones, and provides an indispensable supplement to the Inventory of Greek Coin Hoards and previous volumes of Coin Hoards. $80

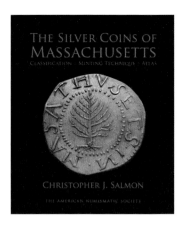

The Silver Coins of Massachusetts by Christopher J. Salmon (2010). ISBN-13: 978-0-89722-316-0. 293 pages, Hardcover. The Silver Coins of Massachusetts is a splendidly illustrated review of the first coins struck in British North America, a mere generation after the establishment of the Massachusetts Bay Colony, employing the latest historical and numismatic evidence as well as novel scientific analysis. $95

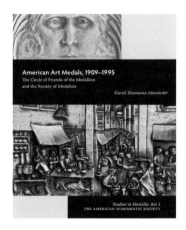

American Art Medals, 1909-1995 by David T. Alexander. ISBN-13: 978-0-89722-317-1. 294 pages, Hardcover. The first comprehensive study of the two most important series of art medals produced in the United States: the medals of the Circle of Friends of the Medallion (1909–1915) and those of the Society of Medalists (1930–1995). Together, these two series offer an unmatched panorama of American medallic sculpture in the twentieth century. $150.

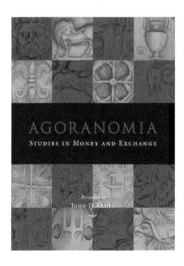

Agoranomia: Studies in Money and Exchange, Presented to John H. Kroll edited by Peter G. van Alfen (2006). ISBN-13: 978-0-89722-298-3. 290 pages, 14 plates, Hardcover. Essays on Greek coinage, exchange, and polis economies from the Archaic to Hellenistic periods, presented to John H. Kroll on his retirement from the University of Texas at Austin. $125

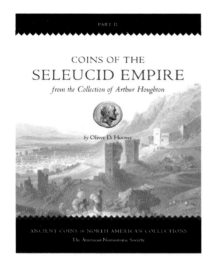
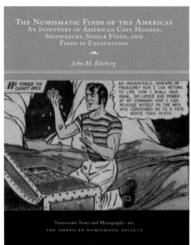